By Nick Bollettieri

With Barry McDermott

NICK BOLLETTIERI'S JUNIOR TENNIS

SIMON AND SCHUSTER
New York

Copyright © 1984 by Nick Bollettieri
All rights reserved
including the right of reproduction
in whole or in part in any form
Published by Simon and Schuster
A Division of Simon & Schuster, Inc.
Simon & Schuster Building
Rockefeller Center
1230 Avenue of the Americas
New York, New York 10020

SIMON AND SCHUSTER and colophon are registered trademarks
of Simon & Schuster, Inc.

Designed by Stanley S. Drate/Folio Graphics Co. Inc.

Manufactured in the United States of America

10 9 8 7 6 5 4 3 2 1

Library of Congress Cataloging in Publication Data
Bollettieri, Nick.
  Nick Bollettieri's Junior tennis.

  Includes index.
  1. Tennis for children. 2. Tennis. 3. Tennis—
Study and teaching. I. McDermott, Barry, II. Title.
III. Title: Junior tennis.
GV1001.4.C45B64   1984   796.342'088054   84-10618

ISBN: 0-671-50840-7

ACKNOWLEDGMENTS

I would like to extend my deepest thanks to Barry McDermott for his enthusiasm, his belief in our ideals, and for capturing the spirit of not only the Academy but of Nick Bollettieri; Don Hutter, Vice President and Senior Editor of Simon & Schuster, the fabulous editor whose confidence from the beginning and guidance throughout made this dream a reality; Sam McCleery, who was so instrumental in getting us together with Simon & Schuster; my son, Jimmy Bollettieri, for the time and talent expended on nearly each and every photo in this book—they are incredible; Ted Meekma for his ideas, patience, support and all the late nights we put in on this project; Julio Moros, my close friend and confidant for so many years; my wonderful family—Mom, Dad, and Rita, Jimmy, my daughters, Danielle, Angel, and Nicole; my beloved wife and best friend, Kellie; the Hurowitz, Landow, and Bassett families, whose friendship and loyalty I will always treasure; the entire staff of the NBTA, the most dedicated and hardworking group of people in the world; and finally, to all those students who at one time or another have been a part of the "Bollettieri system"—without you, it would have all been impossible.

I would like to take this space to recognize some of the many juniors, collegians, and pros who have trained here over the years:

FEMALES

PROS

Carling Bassett
Lisa Bonder
Andrea Temasvari
Pam Casale
Raffaella Reggi
Anne White
Terry Phelps
Kathleen Horvath
Shelley Solomon
Anna Maria Fernandez
Lea Antonoplis
Amy Holton
Kathy Holton
Laura Arraya
Beth Herr
Ann Minter
Barbie Bramblett
Bernadett Randall

COLLEGE

Patricia Hy
Patty Fendick
Gretchen Rush
Jill Smoller
Jill Hetherington

JUNIORS

Michelle Torres
Marianne Wedel
Melissa Brown
Ginny Purdy
Anna Ivan
Jennifer Fuchs
Susan Sloane
Liz Levinson
Ei Iida
Amy Schwartz
Ann Grossman
Dierdre Herman
Jennifer Young
Kelly Boyse
Shiho Okada

MALES

PROS

Jimmy Arias
Brian Gottfried
Yannick Noah
Jimmy Brown
Aaron Krickstein
Tim Mayotte
Eric Korita
Chip Hooper
Rodney Harmon
Mike De Palmer
Pablo Arraya
Fritz Buehning
Vince Van Patten
Brad Gilbert
Eric Fromm
Lloyd Bourne
John Van Nostrand
Andy Kohlberg
Gabriel Urpi

COLLEGE

Paul Annacone
Johnny Levine
Kelly Evernden
Bobby Blair
Tom Fontana
Ril Baxter
Bobby Banck

JUNIORS

Dan Nahirny
John Fleurian
John Boytim
Brian Page
Cary Cohenour
Brian Flowers
Andre Agassi
Martin Blackman
David Kass
Jeff Hersh
Al Parker
Chris Garner
Robby Weiss
Joey Blake

DEDICATION

This book is dedicated to Mr. and Mrs. Louis Marx and Mr. and Mrs. Samuel Reed. My good friends. When I yelled "Help," they said "How?"

CONTENTS

PART FOUR

Tournaments

FOREWORD

Andrea Jaeger was the first person ever to tell me about Nick Bollettieri. She was 13 years old, a sprite in pigtails, and on the court these steely eyes. I had never seen anything like her. She was this little kid, but could she hit a tennis ball! Junior tennis? I, like most of the rest of the country, had only a cursory knowledge of the tots side of the game. This was the late seventies. We all, more or less, assumed that phenoms like Bjorn Borg or John McEnroe or Tracy Austin just seemed to happen. One day they appeared on our television screens and began winning Wimbledon. Who knew where they came from?

Anyway, Jaeger told me about Nick Bollettieri. I was flabbergasted. Kids living at a camp for nine months, going to school in the mornings, then practicing tennis the rest of the day? It sounded preposterous.

Months later I contacted Nick. Over the telephone, his enthusiasm came through loud and clear. The next day, a secretary at the *Sports Illustrated* office phoned me at home. She was worried. A large package had arrived by express mail. It looked important. When I opened it I found reams of promotional material, of newspaper and magazine clips. It was my first introduction to the Nick Bollettieri style. One of his cardinal rules is, Never make a list, do it first.

When I arrived in Sarasota, at the Colony Beach Hotel, I was astounded at what I saw. Kids filled the courts—all sizes and ages, hitting tennis balls pell-mell. Instructors stood alongside grocery carts loaded with tennis balls and fed them to the players, who ripped them back over the net. Hurry, hurry, hurry seemed the order of the day. No time to waste. Wimbledon was waiting.

Orchestrating this operation was Bollettieri, the ex-paratrooper who has never taken no for an answer. He stood on the courts, hunched over like a man worried about helicopter blades overhead, yelling out instructions, never missing a thing. "Jimmy. Hit through the ball. Through the ball. Carling. Over the net. Never into the net." He made a forehand error sound like a crime.

Nick has come a long way since then, and so have a lot of his kids. Jimmy Arias and Carling Bassett now are two of the top players on the men's and women's circuits. No more tots. And Nick has his own operation: the Nick Bollettieri Tennis Academy in Bradenton, Fla. And here is the secret to his success: He is able to take a kid who knows it all—and still teach him more.

Vince Lombardi is one of his heroes. Bollettieri grew up in Pelham, N.Y., the son of a pharmacist, and his neighborhood was the rough-and-tumble type that makes you a fighter. In Pelham, Bollettieri was one of the hardheads and wise guys. He had all of the answers, even before you could think of the questions.

Guys like Nick wound up in the paratroops. Gung-ho! Geronimo!! "Lt. Nicholas Bollettieri. 187th Airborne Division. Yes, sir!" Nick, who had picked up the game of tennis while attending Spring Hill College in Mobile, Alabama, fooled around with tennis and coached a bit while in the service. He got into more serious tennis instruction during a stint at the University of Miami law school and eventually dropped out to devote all his time to tennis. Nick was the head pro at a couple of city courts in North Miami Beach, giving lessons for $1.50 a half-hour. In those days, Nick hardly knew the difference between a Western and a Continental grip. His students would say they wanted a lesson on volleying and Nick would race to Slim Harbett, the most experienced pro in the Miami area, ask him a few questions, and hurry back to the courts to impart his wisdom.

How anyone who has never won a tournament could eventually become the top tennis professor in the world is a story that would mist the eyes of Vince Lombardi. Nick discovered Brian Gottfried, and vice versa. Together, as Nick moved from one club-pro job to the next, they headed for the top, inseparable and consumed by their respective ambitions. "He could make you feel as if you could fly," Gottfried says now.

Nick started in earnest, though still on a shoestring, at the Colony Beach Hotel and Tennis Resort. This was after he had taken a financial bath in a series of camps for adults, and had left a cushy job in Puerto Rico. At the Colony, he invited Anne White, then a promising junior, to come down from her West Virginia home for nine months of intensive training. That was the beginning. Soon his house was overflowing, and his assistant pros were housing kids in their apartments, often without the knowledge of the management, which had no-children clauses in the leases. It was a vagabond operation.

In those early days Nick was considered a lightweight, dismissed by the Establishment (tennis subspecies) because he had not grown up on a country club veranda sipping lemonade and discussing Don Budge's backhand. Who was this character with the hollow, bloodshot eyes and a hoarse voice that sounded like meat left out in the hot sun for days, then buffed with sandpaper? Do you know that his office is in a BROOM CLOSET? Reeally? You don't say.

But as his operation grew, as more and more kids arrived and the tournament victories began piling up, suddenly people began taking another look at the old paratrooper. "Nick Bollettieri, Guest Lecturer" became a familiar line on seminar programs.

Bollettieri came up the hard way, which often is the best way. It probably is easier to ace John McEnroe than it is to fool Nick. He knows people. He reads their service motion, and cuts off their passing shots at the net. Surprisingly sympathetic and tender with his students, he has never forgotten what it is like to be a kid, to have dreams. At his camp, he asks the students to trade in their childhoods on a chance to be great. No one complains that they are not getting a fair exchange.

What Nick has to say can be applied beyond tennis. It can be related to almost any activity involving parents and their children, from sports to academics. He's a teacher, with a string of credentials. Can Nick Bollettieri help your child? Hey, you only have to look at how he has helped himself.

—BARRY McDERMOTT

INTRODUCTION

Over a quarter of a century ago, when I started out in this game, "junior tennis" meant something completely different from what it means now. Back in those days there were a few tournaments for kids, but everything was loosely organized. It was a mom-and-pop operation, except that mom and pop drove to the country club, often with a chauffeur. Now it all has changed. The juniors have a worldwide tournament circuit, with computer rankings, and in some cases—particularly in the European countries, where no distinction is made between the professional and the amateur—there even is prize money. Also, equipment manufacturers such as Prince, the racquet company, Ellesse, the Italian tenniswear firm, and Nike, which makes tennis shoes, are engaged in strong competition to have the kids use their products. In fact, every one of the above firms endorses the Nick Bollettieri Tennis Academy in Bradenton, Fla., and contributes scholarship money to its operation. These firms, along with companies such as Subaru, Penn, and *World Tennis* magazine, and major benefactors such as Mr. and Mrs. Monte Horowitz, Nate Landow, and John Bassett, have helped us to become the no. 1 junior tennis teaching facility in the world.

Number 1. I like that. It rolls off the tongue so nicely. Right now I say that tennis is on its way to becoming the world's no. 1 sport of the young. That may sound preposterous, but consider. . . . It's a global sport. Carling Bassett is from Canada, Yannick Noah from France, Guillermo Vilas from Argentina. Already countries such as China are producing young tennis champions. Sweden, Czechoslovakia, Israel—they all have national tennis centers where kids can go for intense training. Tennis players keep going, day to day, week to week, year to year. And tennis is a game of spectacular tournaments: Wimbledon, the U.S. Open, the French Open.

This outbreak of tennis fever had its genesis in the fitness boom back in the early seventies. Tennis for adults took off, which in turn pushed the professional game to new heights.

That led to an escalation in prize money, tournament television, endorsement contracts, and exhibitions; suddenly tennis, a sport that had been lagging behind its blood cousin, golf, was producing young million-dollar-a-year players such as Martina Navratilova and Jimmy Connors.

Junior tennis has exploded, but even now the realities of junior tennis are largely misunderstood. I want this to become its handbook, a blueprint for success. I want it to be read and used by everyone involved in this new world of junior tennis—the players, the parents, the coaches. Some parts of the book apply more to one of these types of reader than others. Chapters Three and Four, for example, are for parents only. When we get to Part Two—the fundamentals of physical conditioning, strokes, and drills—we have players and coaches in mind, and those parents who (after reading Chapters Three and Four) still want to involve themselves in their children's tennis program. In Part Three, what we call "The Years to Greatness," Chapters Eight through Ten, dealing as they do with children from ages eight to twelve, are addressed for the most part to parents. And from there on, we're talking mainly to the players.

You young readers have picked a game in which the thrill of competition can be with you every day. And if you become a tournament player you will have the opportunity to travel, perhaps around the world. This game can take you places you only dream about. It can take you as far as you let it. I'm going to show you how. We're going to tell you about the strokes, but there's a lot more to the game than good form. In fact there's no such thing as one right or proper form. You only have to look at the games of the top competitors of the last decade—Jimmy Connors, Bjorn Borg, and John McEnroe—to see that none of them have similar styles. They do, however, have one thing in common: They are champions. They have tapped some source that I believe is inside all of us: the ability to do our best under pressure. And that more than anything else is what this book is about. For parents and their children, it will tell all you ever wanted to know about winning. It will give you insights into the game. It will give you formulas for success, and it will explore the world of junior tennis as it can be seen only from the inside. Above all, it will challenge you as a junior player. Do you think you can meet that challenge? We'll see. My payoff from this book will come 10 years or so from now, when I am sitting in the

Friends Box at Wimbledon. I want to look out on that court. I expect it will still be grass, perfectly manicured, and before me will be two competitors locked in struggle. The world will be watching. Hopefully, at least one of those players will be someone who has read what I have written and taken those lessons and put them to good use. It could be you.

Remember: Don't let Nick down and you won't let down yourself. Listen to what I have learned in the 27 years that tennis has been the major influence in my life. Twenty-seven years . . . I hope you will get as much out of reading about them and what they've taught me as I did living them.

ONE

The Bollettieri Way

1978: First year of the full-time Academy, then at the Colony Beach Hotel and Tennis Resort. Nick on the far right; Jimmy Arias, lower right-hand corner; Anne White in center, wearing white shirt; Mike DePalmer, fifth from right, top row; and Pablo Arraya, far right second row (behind Jimmy). Not present: Rodney Harmon and Kathleen Horvath.

1

THE ACADEMY

It's about five hours from Miami to Sarasota, through the Everglades and up the west coast of Florida on U.S. 41, an interminable stretch of highway. When I made that trip in 1975, traveling in a borrowed car to yet another job interview, I was a little depressed and uncertain about my future. Here I was, 42 years old, a tennis pro for over two decades, a hard worker by anyone's standards, and my career, to put it into tennis terms, was like that of a player struggling to get through the qualifying rounds on the satellite circuit. True, I had enjoyed some success, but nothing like I wanted, nothing like I had envisioned when I started.

Julio Moros, my right-hand man still, was with me on that trip. Today he tells people, "All we had for luggage was Nick's name, and it was not a very big name!"

Now I sometimes find myself standing back and catching my breath as I look around the Nick Bollettieri Tennis Academy in Bradenton, Fla. Some people call it a tennis factory. I prefer to think of it as a finishing school. We have everything you need to build champions (just add water, seasoning, and let simmer under the sun about six hours a day). There are 42 outdoor courts and four indoor. Our students are housed in five townhouse buildings, and we have another under construction. There is a Nautilus training center, a swimming pool, a library/study hall, two cafeterias—the list goes on. But our greatest component is people. I like to say that from numbers come good players, and from good players come great players. We have 200 full-time students from around the world and working relationships with many of the top players on the men's and women's circuits.

But all of that was in the future as Julio and I plowed on toward the Colony Beach Hotel and Tennis Resort. I had left my job as director of tennis at the Dorado Beach resort in Puerto Rico, where I had worked for 17 years, and a combination of factors had led to the collapse of All-American Sports, a series of adult tennis camps with which I had worked. Brian Gottfried, my protégé and good buddy, was all grown now, with a family, and competing on the pro circuit. We kept in touch, but it was not like the old days, when he and I traveled together during the summers, fine-tuning his game. Julio is right—he and I did not have much luggage.

Somehow I convinced Dr. Murph Klauber, the owner of the Colony, that I was the man to run his tennis operation. Dr. Klauber was an orthodontist from Buffalo and his vision was to make the Colony one of the outstanding resorts in Florida, using tennis as its centerpiece. I thought we would make a good team.

My primary interest always had been teaching kids. For years, I had operated a summer tennis camp at Wayland Academy in Beaver Dam, Wis., developing many of the teaching theories and drills we still use today: Hurry, hurry, hurry. Keep moving. Don't go for the lines. Hit deep, not into the net. Punch that volley. Low-to-high on your groundstrokes. Hit up on the serve. Come to the net, force your opponent. That sort of stuff. It was the same thing when, together with Hy Zausner, I had founded the Port Washington Tennis Academy outside of New York City, a facility that would eventually produce such champions as Vitas Gerulaitis and John McEnroe.

We started out at the Colony training local kids. By the next season, we had acquired a small reputation and had purchased a tennis club in nearby Bradenton with a new partner, Mike DePalmer, whose two children, Michelle and Mike, Jr., also were promising players. To this core group we added Anne White, inviting her down from her home in Charleston, W.Va. She moved into Mr. DePalmer's house.

The Colony guests loved to watch the young kids work out after school. To the adults, it was like seeing a magic show. The students hit the ball so hard! *Pa-pa-pow*, I always say. *Pa-pa-pow.* Go for it. Kids have no fear, unless they're taught it, either by someone else or through experience. That is why children are wonderful learners. They have no preconceived bias against failure. The road to the top consists of one step

Brian Gottfried.

backward for every three steps forward, and when you become afraid of the backward steps, that's when you are likely to stop progressing.

In August of 1978, when I returned to the Colony after spending the summer at my Beaver Dam camp, I had a little surprise for Julio Moros.

"Get ready for twenty-five students coming down here full-time next month," I said.

"That's great, Nick," answered Julio. "Now where are they going to live?"

"I did my job getting them here," I said. "It's your job finding them a place to stay."

Julio went to work, as did the rest of the staff. In fact we all worked for nine months without a day off. Like I tell the kids now, "No one said it would be easy." It's not easy on them, and it is not easy for us on the teaching side. When a young man walks into my office and asks me for a job as a tennis instructor, there's one way for him to end the interview almost before it starts. "What are my hours?" are the fatal words.

From the beginning, the tennis program was fantastic. Even now, the easiest part of my job is the teaching. The hardest part is contending with outside influences. Which is why we have such a tough code of discipline. We've relaxed some of our standards a bit through trial and error over the years, like dropping the ban against the kids using the telephone except with permission, but we still firmly believe that the more concentration we can provide for our students, the better they will be.

Some have called us a tennis boot camp. I can live with that. Tennis is a unique sport. Where else can you be a millionaire by 17, as Andrea Jaeger was on the women's circuit? The pressure is on from a young age, a time when youngsters are notorious for poor concentration. A tennis career is fragile—like a flash of light: *poof*, here and then gone. So why not train hard? Why not give up a few things for a chance to be great? People say I ask the kids to sacrifice. I say, "What sacrifice?" Ask Jimmy Arias, or Carling Bassett. Talk to Anne White, Rodney Harmon, Pablo Arraya, Kathleen Horvath, Eric Korita, or Pam Casale. See if they feel as if they have missed anything because of their dedication to tennis. They all were in our first group of students. Now they are on the pro circuit. From numbers come good players. From good players come great players. That's the formula for success.

When my kids walked into junior tournaments in those early years, the other players looked at them as if the Marines had landed. We had discipline. We had respect.

The kids thrived in this environment. Jimmy Arias's mother used to call him all the time when he first arrived. "When are you coming home?" she would ask him. If reporters were around, doing stories on the camp, Jimmy would tell them, "I don't have the heart to tell her that I don't want to come home."

Early on I realized the importance of treating everyone equally. There was one infamous incident involving Jimmy. Without question, Jimmy was the camp star. He was just a little better than the other boys, this spider of a kid, all arms and legs and skinny body, who could absolutely crunch a forehand. He also had a bit of mischief about him. Nothing serious. Just Nick Bollettieri about three decades younger. He had a habit of bouncing his racquet on the court if he hit a bad shot. "No bouncing your racquet," I must have yelled at him a thousand times. One day I saw him miss a shot, then hit his racquet on the ground. Three courts over, I took off like a man possessed, charged up to him, grabbed the racquet out of his hands, and yelled, "Here, you want to bounce your racquet? Let's really bounce it!" With that I smashed it on the ground. Jimmy was incredulous! "Nick," he said plaintively, "that was my favorite racquet." It taught him a lesson. I don't think Jimmy ever again bounced his racquet on the court.

We had a big responsibility to parents. They had given us their children. I remember the first time I saw Carling Bassett. She showed up with her father, John, now a good friend and a wonderful supporter of the Academy. But back then, he was just another parent. They arrived at the Colony one afternoon. John Bassett asked me to hit with his daughter.

Carling then was only 11 years old, a thin little board of a kid with braces on her teeth. But quickly I saw that she was a player. *Pa-pa-pow!* The ball flew across the net. She put everything into it.

We finished and I walked over to her father. "She's great," I told him.

He looked at Carling, who had this eager, expectant look on her face. Then he turned back to me. "She's yours," he said.

By September of '79 our reputation had grown such that we had 100 students living with us. Arrangements had been made with the Bradenton Academy for the kids to get their

Carling Bassett and Nick, 1978.

schooling, from 7:30 to 12:00 every morning. (Today we also use the St. Stephen's Episcopal School.) We had purchased an old motel in Bradenton, renovated it, and used it as sleeping accommodations for the kids. We hired a full-time chef, expanded the kitchen and dining facilities, and acquired a 66-passenger bus, as well as a van and a truck.

Everyone was caught up in the enthusiasm. Some evenings, I would pay an unexpected visit to the camp dormitory and find one of the students' parents, surrounded by a bunch of other kids. They would be looking at a videotape of the day's workout.

Still, we needed more and more room. Finally, in 1980, with the help of my friend Louis Marx, our dream came true and we moved to our present facility. This time, Julio will tell you, we brought a whole bunch of luggage.

We had no blueprint for success in those first years. What we realized was that each young person is different. We tried to fit the system to the players, not vice versa. There is no guaranteed recipe for Tennis Champion Souffle.

Obviously, not everyone can be a champion; for every winner, there must be a loser. But the lessons you learn on the tennis court serve you well in life. We mention the great tournament records of our players because obviously they are an endorsement of our system, but I guarantee you that our players who have decided against careers in pro tennis also have put to good use the lessons they have learned at the Academy. They've learned not to bounce their racquets, to give that little extra, to sacrifice and fight hard. They've grown up, and we've grown right along with them.

At the Academy: welcome to the NBTA (right); Nick overlooking his 46 courts (below), with indoor center left, behind library and office. Facing page: running the lines, pushups for dessert, and then Nautilus.

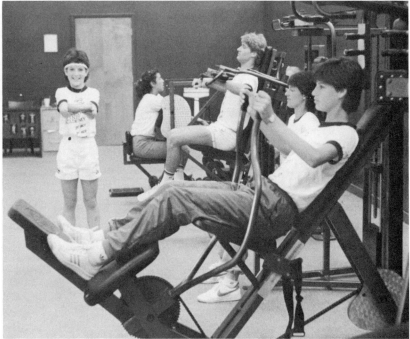

2

A GAME FOR CHAMPIONS

I love tennis. I love it professionally the way architects admire their drawings or accountants take pride in their ledgers. I love it as art, which is nothing less than what it is when played at its highest level—genius uncovered, competition that hints at the reserves of the human spirit. You need guts to play this game. You need a brain, a plan of attack, and the will to stick to it. You need physical strength, reflexes, temerity. And you don't walk alone.

No tennis player has ever made it completely on his or her own, and none ever will. Whether it was a young Jimmy Connors, taught at the knee of his mother, Gloria, or John McEnroe, tutored by former Mexican Davis Cupper Tony Palafox, or Yannick Noah, spotted as a child by Arthur Ashe at Noah's home in the French Cameroons and brought to France for training by Philippe Chartier, the head of that country's tennis federation—no matter who, every champion has had someone to draw out his or her talent.

I admit that I'm a fanatic, that I'm oblivious to the world outside tennis. I don't know the names of the top television programs, or much about politics, and I don't read much. But I know this game of tennis. I can watch pro Fritz Buehning, a student of mine since he was a gregarious, chubby little kid, and see that he is having trouble serving because he is shifting the ball in his fingers on his toss, or tell the French junior, John Fleurian, a visitor to the academy, that he needs more shoulder rotation on his serve. Or I'll go nuts when I see young Eric Korita dog a passing shot. "Hit the ball, Eric," I'll yell. "Don't baby it." And Eric will get this silly grin on his face. But you watch the next time he has a passing shot, and how he tees off on it.

Nick in his teaching crouch, Jimmy Arias listening.

I keep an eye on things, especially the fundamentals. Never lose your fundamentals, the foundation of tennis. Likewise, I have to watch and continue to take care of the little things. So out on the practice courts at the Academy there are telephones. I stand there, one eye on the students, the phone up to my ear, talking to people around the world, yet never missing anything with the kids. Sometimes I wonder what the people on the phone think when suddenly I yell, "His grip is wrong. Tell 'im to get his hand over more."

People say that champions are born, not made. That's a cynic's view, the easy way out. I say champions are discovered, like nuggets in a vein of ore. No one knows who the best player in the world is, because the best player is a kid who hasn't yet picked up a racquet, or one who hasn't had the resources to play. To illustrate my point, one of the top college basketball stars today is Akeem Olajawon of the University of Houston. He was born and raised in Nigeria. It was only good fortune that he played the sport that made him famous. How many potential tennis champions are there in Nigeria, or in China, Calgary, or the New York City ghettos? How many kids waiting to be discovered, waiting to be found and developed?

Jerry Kramer, an offensive guard for Vince Lombardi when the Green Bay Packers were the masters of pro football, once commented about his coach, "I don't believe anyone knows what they can do until they try . . . and Lombardi makes sure you try." You find a child and get him to try, to commit himself to a goal, to discipline himself for a later reward. That's when you see magic.

Tennis is a simple game. How else could children play it so well? These kids come right out of the juniors and make their marks in the record books. You don't see 16-year-old basketball players in the National Basketball Association. Or teenage golfers winning the Masters tournament. There are no high school kids good enough to quarterback the Dallas Cowboys. On the other hand, tennis is very difficult, a game that involves enormous discipline. That's the problem a parent or coach faces. How do you instill discipline in a child, someone whose entire existence has been so short that a month seems like an eternity?

But I make you this promise. Take a child and involve him in a plan for greatness—what we at the Academy call "The Program"—and he will go to college on a tennis scholarship. At the least. To some, that may seem a preposterous statement. Our results suggest otherwise. I say that you can challenge a child, goad her to reach further than she thinks she can reach. You may not make a champion, but I know you'll make a winner. I know you can teach youngsters lessons of discipline and courage that will stay with them for a lifetime.

Learning to conquer fear is something you learn forever. I know that as well as anyone. I made 95 jumps as a paratrooper, and on every one I closed my eyes, scared blue when I stepped up to that door—but I jumped, because I had to. Last year, 16-year-old Aaron Krickstein joined me in Florence, Italy, for the beginning of his first summer on the pro circuit. He was frightened, sure. Who wouldn't be? We were at the tournament site at 7:30 A.M. for practice. The courts weren't even open, so we went over to a backboard and worked on footwork drills. My son, Jimmy, took photographs, and in them you can see the uncertainty in Aaron's face. But he jumped. He had to. And that summer made him a man. In September he defeated Vitas Gerulaitis at the U.S. Open and set the tennis world buzzing with the power of his groundstrokes.

When you involve your children in tennis you give them a game for the rest of their lives, a tool for happiness. Many of the teaching pros and assistants who work with me in my camps are former students. We're like a family. Some of my staff started with me as ballboys in Puerto Rico when I taught during the winters at the Dorado Beach resort. They came from poverty. As I did. Sure, I know what it is to look through the fence at a tennis court. I came up on the outside looking in, not part of the Establishment. But ultimately all the work I was forced to do to become accepted, all the extra hours I put in, the dues I paid—it all made me a better teacher. My students believe in me because they know that nothing has come easy for me either. I know when they look over and see me at a tournament that they feel a little better. They understand I have been willing to work and pay the price. If you show a child by example, he or she will follow.

All of my students are different, yet all are similar in one important way: They have a love for competition. True, in some it's more powerful than in others, but all of them have it, or else they wouldn't be here. There are levels of the game, but few people understand them—how to progress from one level to another, how to move up the rungs. The secret is your ability to tough out the low spots. Never have a disastrous day of practice; end it on a high note. Always fight the rough times. Never give in or capitulate. Never lose sight of your objectives. I can't tell you how many times I heard backroom gossip that Jimmy Arias "wouldn't make it." We can laugh about it now. People thought he was too small, that his backhand was too weak, that his serve-and-volley game never would be big league. Today he is the fifth-ranked player in the world, at 19 years of age. And he is *not* satisfied.

Every top player has fantastic work habits. Many people think that the better a person plays, the better he concentrates. I say it is the other way around. People forget that three years ago it looked as if Jimmy Connors, then 29 years old, was finished as a threat in major championships. He was all but written off. Bjorn Borg was dominating him, John McEnroe was coming up, seemingly destined to reign as no. 1 for the next decade. And there was a bunch of new kids on the block, immense talents such as Ivan Lendl, Jose-Luis Clerc, and Johan Kriek. But I knew Connors was far from finished when, one night at the U.S. Open in Flushing Meadows, I saw him come loping out of the gloom. I was on a back court at

Nick and Aaron in Florence, Italy, 1983.

the tournament, watching some friends play an informal match. An hour or so earlier, Connors had dispatched an opponent in an early round. Now the place was deserted. But here came Jimmy, his hair plastered across his wet forehead, jogging. Months before he had committed himself to an exercise program to build up his stamina. When he was younger and naturally fit, he could run down any ball. Now, uncharacteristically looking up in the rankings, he was determined to work. Connors went on to win two U.S. Open titles and a Wimbledon championship, and regain his ranking as the best player in the world.

That is the type of discipline I am talking about. Last year at the U.S. Open, Jimmy Arias stood in a corner of the Stadium Court and held a towel to his face while I wondered what was wrong. He was wobbling. The temperature at the Open that week was close to 100 degrees. The courts were like blacktop, all but bubbling. Arias later would tell me that he felt delirious, that he could barely concentrate enough to recall his own name. Little did we know that he was coming down with mononucleosis, an illness that would sideline him for three months after the Open.

"C'mon, Jimmy," I yelled to him from my seat in the stands. "Be tough, Jimmy." I knew something was wrong. He was down two sets to one in his fourth-round match with Sweden's Joachim Nystrom, a baseliner who can run down balls all day. It looked as if Jimmy's tournament was going to end right here. "C'mon, Jimmy," I yelled as he poured ice water over his head. "Don't give up."

Suddenly, in the next two sets, Arias started playing a brand of tennis that few people there had ever seen. *Pa-pa-pow.* He fought back, blasting his forehand from corner to corner. Now it was Nystrom who was on the ropes. Jimmy won the fourth set, 6–0—a bagel job! And he was just as spectacular in the fifth, spraying winners all over. He won that set 6–0, too. It was unbelievable. Twelve straight games won after being on the verge of collapse! How easy it would have been for him in his weakened condition to cave in two hours earlier, to walk off the court or to play only halfheartedly in that fourth set when he was facing elimination. He had an excuse sitting there nice and plump, all ready to be used. Instead he buckled down and came back. I say it is because he had a reservoir of strength inside him, a pool that had been filled over the years. That's what I mean when I yell at my students to do a little extra, to give a little more. I also tell them, "It'll help you."

That week at the U.S. Open, Jimmy Arias went on, despite his physical condition, to reach the semifinals of the tournament. In the quarters, he beat reigning French Open champion Yannick Noah in a night match. And at its conclusion, Jimmy threw his racquet 50 feet into the air in celebration. I think it was the only time he ever threw his racquet that I didn't yell at him. What the heck, let the kid have a little fun.

3

YOU BE THE PARENT, I'LL BE THE COACH

In the next two chapters, we're going to talk about the most maligned group in junior tennis. We all know the stereotype of the pushy tennis parent, the one on the sidelines yelling criticisms at his or her child. What you probably don't know, however, is the pressure the parents of juniors often find themselves subjected to. There are so many decisions, and so much riding on the outcomes. The stakes are incredibly high. One day a child is a gawky teenager. The next she is standing before royalty at Wimbledon.

We're going to talk now about some of the common problems a tennis parent faces. The dilemma of a father who tries to put some distance between himself and his child's junior career, while keeping the family unit intact. The decision whether to coach your child or to delegate the responsibility to a competent tennis professional. How to keep your child interested in the game. And, if you decide to coach your child, little guidelines that may help you steer clear of the rough spots.

Let's make two things clear at the start: Every child needs parents, and every tennis player needs a coach. I'm not sure the two should be the same. Some parents do it, and for many it has worked. The results can be great. Jimmy Connors, taught by his mother, Gloria. Chris Evert, pointed in the right direction by her father, Jim. Gene and Sandy Mayer, trained by their father, Alex. Of course, all of these parents were experienced teaching pros. That's a fact often lost on other ambitious parents. It's so easy, so tempting to think that you

It's hard not to get involved.

can be the power behind your child's tennis, that your advice can point them toward greatness. Beware—nearly always it's a trap. Know what you are getting into.

First of all, you'll put a tremendous strain on the family. All of your attention will be focused on something that is alien to a family unit: devoting yourself to one child to the exclusion of the others, perhaps also of your spouse. Instead of working together, you will discover that every decision you make, even something as basic as where you'll live or what job you'll hold, even what you eat or how you vacation—everything—will come down to how it affects the tennis of your child. You'll get so caught up and immersed in the trees that you'll forget about the forest. The natural inclination of every parent is to give a child every advantage, to be concerned for the child's welfare. But consider this: You wouldn't attempt to teach your children academics at home. So why would you want to teach them tennis?

Strange things can happen—naturally close relationships can sour, roles get reversed. A few years ago I was at the Orange Bowl juniors tournament in Miami, Fla., observing the girls 16s. I was watching this one player, who was only 14 or 15, struggling on the court. She was a retriever, dogged and determined; her style made her work much harder than her opponent had to. It was a saga as old as tennis: defense versus offense.

An older gentleman was standing nearby, and we began to talk. It turned out that the girl who was working so hard on the court was his daughter. The match continued. During a changeover, the girl approached the man and said, "Get me a Band-Aid!" Her tone was more command than request. The fellow went off to find a Band-Aid.

He returned, and by then his daughter was playing again. Every point took forever. Evidently suffering from blisters on her feet, his daughter doggedly kept the ball in play, her face as grim as a rock. Minutes passed. There was a changeover. Her father forgot about the Band-Aid in his pocket. Then there was another changeover. His daughter approached and stood in front of him. Her face took on a look of exasperation. She began tapping her foot, her hands on her hips. Then she started to shake her head as if to say, Can you believe how dumb this guy is? Finally, her voice filled with sarcasm, she blurted out, "Well? Where is it?" The man remembered the Band-Aid. Frantic, he started fumbling, checking his pockets. He couldn't find it. He was confused. His daughter stood tapping her foot in agitation, sighing to the world. Finally the man found the bandage and handed it to her. She snatched it away, clearly disgusted. Chastised, the man sat before her meekly as she applied the Band-Aid to her foot. As she rose and started back onto the court, he started to offer some mild encouragement. She turned on him, her face sullen. "Shut up," she said.

I was appalled. This man loved his daughter—in fact, loved her so much that when she told him to shut up, he had nothing to say, nothing left in him. Some time ago, a decision had been made to devote every consideration to his daughter. Every decision was hers. Tennis had taken over. And she had taken over the family.

I recall, at another junior tournament, sitting in the clubhouse and discussing a player who suddenly went from champion to has-been, at the age of 14. I was speaking about him with the father of one of the top juniors in the country. He taught his son. In fact, he had uprooted the family and moved to California so the boy could have the best practice facilities. As we spoke, it appeared to me that this man had a reasoned and perceptive approach to his son's tennis. He spoke of how they had mapped out realistic goals, how they spoke often about pressure, how they communicated. Talking about the player who had burned out at a young age, this man said,

"The father lost sight of what they were trying to do. I won't let that happen. You cannot get too caught up in tennis." Gee, I thought, this guy has it all in perspective. Later that year, I heard that his son wanted to quit tennis. It seems he and his father had had a fistfight in the lobby of a hotel at a junior tournament.

I bring up these horror stories because too often parents have no idea what they are getting into when they decide to coach their children. I am a coach. I am also a parent with four children: Jimmy, Jr., who is 28; Danielle, 17; Angel, 14; and little Nicole. None of my three older children ever became a full-time student of our program. They play tennis, but they play it when and how they want. Years ago, when my tournament kids were crammed into my Thunderbird and crisscrossing the Midwest, going from tournament to tournament, Jimmy came along, not so much to compete as to share in the adventure. Brian Gottfried was in the car. He was a tennis player. Jimmy was my son. The two things never got confused.

Jimmy now is a talented photographer (most of the pictures in this book are his). He also helps run my summer tennis camp in Deerfield, Mass. He's great with the kids. And now that he's an adult, he has a little insight on me, his father. He makes the point that had I not been divorced at the time I took the job as director of tennis at the Colony Hotel, the Academy probably never would have come into being. It's a good point. I wouldn't have had the time to devote both to marriage and to all that was needed to build up the program.

I made it as a father because my kids were old enough to understand, and had their own resources, but I'm afraid Jimmy is right. Ultimately I have been married to my life in tennis. I have been to Paris many times and have never set foot in the Eiffel Tower. I have been to Rome just as often and have never visited the Colosseum. I don't have time to stop to sniff the flowers. When I am with my kids at tournaments, it is always the same: up at 7:00 A.M. and let's get going and don't stop until midnight. No outside distractions. How many parents can be equally committed? How many kids would *want* them to be?

Let me tell you about another father. I've told you about Carling Bassett, how her dad, John, dropped her off on my doorstep and gave me the unspoken message: Make her a champion. Carling was a good player at the time. You could see the potential. But she was getting whipped easily by players in the 12-and-under division. Her father knew she needed help.

John Bassett is an athlete. He played Davis Cup tennis for Canada and was one of his country's finest squash players. He is a fierce competitor in a family of competitors. You mention the name John Bassett in Canada and people know you are talking about the Bassetts of Toronto. His father and his father's father, both also named John, built an empire in communications: newspaper publishing, radio and television. That tells you something about the challenge the John Bassett who is Carling's father must have felt at a very young age. He understands great expectations.

Surely, over the years John Bassett has bitten his tongue many times when talking about Carling. Surely, he has caught himself over and over again watching her practice, fighting the urge to tell her what she was doing incorrectly. He has never said a word. But you know what John Bassett has told Carling? "If you want to come home, the door is open. If you want to quit, that's fine."

He has become one of the Academy's greatest supporters and a close friend. One of our practice courts carries a plaque with his name inscribed upon it. John Bassett made his daughter a champion by letting someone else do the job.

Given today's pressures and the rewards available, I say get your child a coach and listen to him. Sometimes children complain that what the coach wants them to do is not right. Maybe it doesn't "feel right." Maybe it is too difficult. Believe me, tennis may look easy, but it's a science as elaborate, as misunderstood, as hard and frustrating to master as any you will find. The old injunction may be trite but it's true: Don't tell me how to run my business and I won't tell you how to run yours.

Quite recently, I had a brief run-in with a father. One of my best students over the years has been Pam Casale. She came to me a little late, with her strokes already more-or-less ingrained. She was not a dominating player in the juniors. But I saw something that you cannot teach: a heart. She was a fighter. She scrapped for every point. She gave up nothing. I liked that.

Pam surprised a lot of people when she turned pro. Just as some basketball players' games become better in the National Basketball Association than they were in college, so did Pam's determination and dogged style help her as a professional. She moved right up in the standings. But then Pam started losing matches I felt she should have won. Something was wrong. About this time, her father telephoned me with an idea. Pam's weaknesses have always been obvious: Her backhand isn't classical; she doesn't have much of a serve. So her father had a plan. He wanted one of my pros to work with his daughter about two or three hours a day. We would change her backhand. She would develop a big serve. She would become a power player. It seemed so simple. So I listened, even though I felt Pam's father was seeing the trees but not the forest. Pam's weaknesses over the years had forced her to become a scrambler. She had developed into a relentless bulldog of a player. But now, probably because she had been thinking too much about correcting those weaknesses, she had stopped giving the little extra on the court that had made her a winner. To her father it seemed easier to correct the weaknesses than to build upon her strength. Except for one problem. It was too late, much too late in her career to think about revamping her game. She had to play the hand she was dealt. So finally I said, "Mr. Casale, if your daughter does not go back to what she has always done—run her tail off for every ball—she has no future in pro tennis."

They were harsh words, but the message came through. Her father bowed out, and a few weeks later Pam beat Hana Mandlikova, the hottest player on the circuit at the time. A few weeks after that, she faced Tracy Austin, the kind of baseliner a player like Pam really has to work to beat. "Get your first serve in," I told her. "Hit every ball down the middle. Make every rally go at least ten strokes." The next night, my secretary, Kathy Owens, came running up to me. Pam was on the phone. She had won the match. You could hear me yell for happiness all over the Academy. That night at a meeting, I told my staff, "That win is worth more than money. That's what makes the Academy worthwhile."

There's a fine line between being a pushy parent and being supportive. The disaster stories are well documented. Take Argentina's Claudia Casabianca, a top junior in the late 1970s. She missed a shot in this one tournament and her father stalked onto the court and slapped her. At the Orange Bowl in 1982, Carling Bassett won the title by forfeit when the mother of her opponent, Manuela Maleeva of Bulgaria, pulled Manuela off the court because she thought the linespeople were making unfair calls.

It poses a quandary when parents are asked to relinquish

control of their children, but I feel it must be done—at least in the area of tennis—if the child is going to progress. A coach cannot have a student's respect if the parents are preempting him and his teaching methods. I don't think Bjorn Borg's parents interfered with Lennart Bergelin when he traveled with Borg. I don't think Jose-Luis Clerc's parents interfere with Pato Rodriguez when he coaches Clerc.

An incident took place at the Academy the other day. Luckily, I was away on a trip, because if I had seen it, I might have collapsed. What happened was a father came onto the court while some players were drilling and he began chewing out his daughter, criticizing her for making mistakes and not concentrating. Everybody was stunned. Gabriel Jaramillo, one of my assistants, stopped the man. "Listen, if Nick was here, he would tell you the same thing I'm going to," Gabriel said. "If you ever come onto the court, if you ever criticize your daughter in front of people, you won't be allowed to set foot on the Academy grounds again. Now go over to the bleachers and sit down and don't move."

When you become overly involved in your child's development as a player, you put pressure on the child that almost has to be counterproductive. The game is tough enough. Lord knows that I'm tough enough. But there is a key difference. If your coach yells at you, you can turn to your parents for comfort. If your parents yell at you, to whom do you turn?

Teaching tennis is easy. Teaching parents is another thing altogether. I joke that parents are my Achilles heel, an apt description since so often they end up underfoot. But with parents who give me autonomy with their children, life is beautiful. I can instill discipline. The child respects my decisions. The progress is fantastic.

I live with my players. They are as much a part of me as I am of them. I see and judge them in a way a parent never could. I don't look at the same things. A father sees his boy; I see a flawed forehand. Once, during a meeting with the students at the Academy, I was criticizing a younger boy whose game was not the strongest in camp because he didn't work as diligently as he should. "You don't even know my name," he said softly. The kid was calling my hand. And he was right. I *didn't* know his name. I'm from the Babe Ruth school of recollection. I occasionally forget the names of people who have been on my staff for years. Now, I looked at the group of students. They were waiting to see what I would do next.

"This is you, Aaron," Nick mimes. Sheepishly, Krickstein takes the advice.

"I want ten kids to stand up," I said.

A group rose. "Okay," I said. "You have a Western forehand. You use an Eastern grip. You play with a Prince. You have a one-hand backhand. You have a two-hander with a one-hand release. . . ." I went right down the line, rattling off the grip, racquet, and playing style of each kid.

"Now, was I wrong?" I asked. Nobody said anything. Then I turned to the kid who had confronted me, and said, "Don't think because I don't call you by name that I don't know you. And don't think that I'm not watching what you do."

As a coach, it's my duty to learn everything I can about all of my students. On some you have to use a hammer. Others need a gentle touch. Some almost have to be embarrassed before they will fight back and try harder. People see me chastising a student and they cluck their tongues: "There's Bollettieri being abusive again." They have no idea what I'm doing. Jeanne Austin, the mother of Tracy, has said that many times Tracy's coach, Robert Lansdorp, pushed Tracy to tears during practice. I've done the same. But when I see one of my students standing as a winner on center court, acknowledging the cheers of the crowd, that's when my eyes start to water. That's when it is all worth it.

4

IF YOU STILL WANT TO DO IT: Goals and Motivation

I'm sure that some of you parents, despite everything I said in the last chapter, still believe you can coach your children. Okay. You can do it. Much of the rest of this book is pretty much based on that assumption—it hands over to you my program for success with children that will help you make winners, maybe champions, of your own kids. In the next section, Part Two, you'll get my fundamentals of conditioning, basic strokes, and drills. After that comes the big journey—a child's progression through the years of development. But for now, let's talk about two more-general considerations, major ingredients of my own success with kids through which parents can really help: instilling and supporting motivation, and setting goals.

Motivating kids is what I do best, probably because I've always been able to motivate myself. When I was a youngster, I was always hustling little jobs around the neighborhood. I sold flowers, worked as a delivery boy, and did other odd jobs. I liked the sound of coins jingling in my pocket.

As an athlete, I was a little better than average, but I probably had as much heart as anyone. I was pretty good in high school football—the small, wiry guy who had the good moves. In college, I discovered tennis, teaching myself to play, and I made the tennis team—not as a star by any means, but I made it. Later, in the Army, in between moments playing John Wayne jumping out of planes, I taught tennis. Still later, when I was in law school down in Miami, I continued to teach a little on the side.

It was apparent that I had the ability to pick up things in other people's games, and I was able to motivate them. I especially liked working with kids. I've always appreciated young people. To this day, most of my friends are younger than myself. My son, Jimmy, says it's because I'm still a kid myself. He's probably right.

Kids are easy to motivate. Just show them what they can be. That's why I always want to have great players around my Academy. What a fantastic example for the youngsters to be able to see Jimmy Arias, Carling Bassett, Aaron Krickstein, Eric Korita, Fritz Buehning, or some of the other tremendous players that work with us!

Kids are basically lazy. I believe that. You do, too, if you're honest. That's what makes them kids. They don't know anything about the lessons of life, about taking knocks and growing up and achieving something. Kids always take the easy way. This insight came to me one day at my summer camp in Beaver Dam when I watched a group of students walk through a partially opened gate. The gate had probably a 15-inch-wide gap, because someone had opened it the wrong way. As I watched about 150 kids squeeze sideways through that gate, rather than taking the split second necessary to open it properly, I thought, "That's why people pay you to teach tennis."

Obviously, many children play tennis more or less for their parents. It's a way of getting parental approval. The kids are introduced to the sport when they tag along to their mother and father's weekly game down at the public courts. When the adults are finished, the children get a few minutes of batting the ball around. Soon, they are eager to play.

This is a great way to pick up the game. The key element is that the child *wants* to play. No one is pushing him or her. I think Andrea Jaeger's burning desire as a tennis player was kindled when she was very young. Her father, Roland, had started Andrea's older sister, Susy, in tennis. Andrea also wanted lessons, but her father felt that she was too small, at seven years of age, to get much out of instruction. So he made a pact. If she would practice on her own against the garage door at the family home in suburban Chicago, practice all winter, then, come spring, he would teach her. Andrea was religious about training against the door. Every evening she would bundle up, put on gloves and go out and bang away. The garage was not heated! Finally one evening she ran into the living room, all excited. "I hit twenty-five straight forehands," she told her father. Roland Jaeger looked at her. "Go hit twenty-six," he said.

Tutoring your child in tennis is like being both the coach of a team and its general manager. On the court, as coach, you will make certain demands. But as general manager of the family, you will have to make other kinds of decisions, too. Your child will put you to the point: Do you want me to practice, or do you want me to cut the grass? When it's a question of family or tennis, let the family come first.

Many children have a common goal when they are very young. They want to beat their parents. That is their Wimbledon. By taking on the role of coach, you put yourself in some jeopardy. You have to ask yourself the same questions you would ask when picking a coach for your child. How extensive is the coach's knowledge of the game? Maybe you don't have to be a good tennis player, but you do have to know the game. This book can help you a lot there. Another question: How does the coach react to the child on the court? Day to day, will he be able to motivate the player, will he inspire obedience? Be honest with yourself—Is that part of your personality, part of your relationship with your child?

In choosing a coach, you also have to ask yourself if his schedule is such that he will be able to give your child the help he or she requires. Is he organized, does he have the time? This is perhaps the biggest question for parents tutoring their own children, especially if they're holding down full-time jobs. If you don't have the time to give your kid the attention needed, don't try.

Occasionally you will find a professional player who has essentially taught himself. It's not something I recommend, but it does happen. Vince Van Patten was winning tournaments long before he had his first tennis lesson, when he was 23! Obviously Vince is a gifted athlete, with fantastic foot speed and reflexes. In 1981 he won the Seiko tournament in Japan, beating John McEnroe and Jose-Luis Clerc. But how much better could Van Patten have been if he had taken lessons as a young kid? We'll never know.

I always had goals. I wanted to be the best pro teaching tennis. Wherever I went, my first question was: "Who's the

Although largely self-taught, Vince Van Patten frequently joins the Academy to improve or refresh his game.

best?" I wanted to beat that person. At Dorado Beach, as tennis director, I drew up master plans so that almost every minute of sunlight could be utilized for tennis during the busy season. I was like an air traffic controller, juggling players between courts. In Puerto Rico, I hung my wet tennis shirts on the back fence so they could dry while I gave another lesson. I kept rotating the shirts. Up with the wet, down with the dry. As I taught, assistants would bring me sandwiches so I could skip taking a break for lunch. I kept records of how many lessons I gave, and the next year I would try to set a new record.

The message I bring my kids, and you must bring to yours, is: Always try to be the best. And the only way to be the best is first to be the best you can be. In other words, first fulfill your potential, *then* you can be the best in the country, or in the world. Don't try to jump from square one to square 10.

From the very first day, the primary goal should be to have fun. End each day on the upbeat. Then, as soon as the youngster begins to understand what tennis may mean to him or her, it's time to sit down for a talk. Simple discussions on what is involved in playing tournaments, in making the high school or college team, even in turning pro may make a student a little more realistic from the beginning. Without destroying hopes and dreams, you can show your youngster that it is a long, hard road to the top and there's not enough room for everyone.

Don't place unrealistic time restrictions on achieving a specific goal. Total success at a young age does not always guarantee a brilliant future. We all know examples of the "young sensations" who win everything early and never fulfill their expectations. John McEnroe, by contrast, never was a dominating player in the juniors. Often it is the student who takes his lumps and experiences success at a slow but steady rate who is better off.

I recently read a story about women professional golfers that underscored what I believe is the proper attitude for parents and their kids to have about sports. Patty Sheehan, now one of the bright young talents on the pro golf circuit, grew up in a family of skiers, and she was one of the best in the country, the type who seemed destined for the Olympics. In fact, she hardly ever lost a race. But she quit when she was 14 because the sport simply was no longer fun. Her father, Bobo, who once was the ski coach for the U.S. Olympic team, didn't badger her about giving up the sport *he* loved. In fact, he was supportive. "In a way," Patty said, "he seemed relieved that I could make a decision like that." The consequence of this was that because her father never had done anything to extinguish the competitive fire that burned in his daughter, she needed an outlet for her athletic desire. She took up golf. The rest is history.

Get yourself a master plan, be flexible, but try to accomplish what you want. Jimmy Arias probably cost himself a chance at the record book by joining my Academy. He had been the national champion in both the 12-and-under and the 14-and-under divisions. When he left Buffalo and came down to live in my house, it meant that he was unable to play in enough local New York tournaments to qualify for national events. Some people thought we were holding him out of the 16s, and then the 18s, because we were afraid he would lose. Actually, it was just too difficult for him to qualify for the tournaments.

The result was that Jimmy was sort of written off as a player. His star fell. One year he went to the Orange Bowl as a seeded player and lost in the first round. He didn't have much of a record in junior tournaments. People thought we were hiding him. Finally, he began playing small satellite events on the pro circuit. In one of his first tournaments, a Penn Circuit event in Miami, he lost in the first round of qualifying to Mark Woolridge, a student at the Academy whom Jimmy beat regularly day to day. You think that night I wasn't depressed? I felt the pressure. But we had a master plan. We stuck with it. We made a major adjustment on Jimmy's backhand, a semi-Western grip allowing for more topspin. By September, Jimmy was playing in the U.S. Open and winning his first big match. The next year he was a regular on the pro circuit.

Last year I approached Lisa Bonder's mother during a pro tournament in Perugia, Italy. Lisa, even though she was only 16, already was on the pro circuit, and doing well. But I could see that she could do much better. I told her mother, "Mrs. Bonder, if Lisa is to become a top player, we've got to make some changes, beginning with that forehand." I took a chance, because if Lisa didn't make it, then it was Nick's fault. I'm not always right, but fortunately I'm right more often than I'm wrong. Lisa came down to the Academy and worked. We lengthened out her follow-through, which helped her when she was nervous. Previously she had stopped the stroke almost on contact, a natural reaction of players under pressure. The longer follow-through gave her a chance to let the racquet flow through the ball. Secondly, I had Lisa watch Jimmy Arias and notice how he accelerates his racquet on contact. Those two little corrections made her forehand the best among my female Academy students. Lisa's ranking over the next months jumped to no. 11 on the pro circuit.

We set down a goal for Lisa, one that I felt was attainable, mapped out a plan, and convinced her that she could accomplish our objectives. Sounds easy, doesn't it? Actually, it only took about a year of practice, 3–4 hours a day.

There's a special consideration you have to take into account if you have more than one child playing tennis seriously. Sibling rivalries are fantastic for developing champions, but almost always, sooner or later, one child will begin to dominate. It is easy to see that that child has more talent—it's just that simple. Obviously, this can inflict a heavy toll on the family. How would you like to be a child and hear one of your parents' friends ask them about you, "Is this the one that plays tennis, or is this the other one?" *The other one.* It sounds almost inhuman.

I may not be one to talk about keeping the family structure in place, about balancing the demands of tennis against the demands of family—I've had more than my share of marital problems. But sometimes there just is not enough love for everyone. So here's one rule: Make sure there are no losers at home.

Set your goals and make them attainable. Achieve them. Set some more goals. Help your child move . . . right . . . up . . . the . . . ladder.

TWO

Fundamen-
tals

5

PHYSICAL CONDITIONING

Tennis has changed so much in the last decade. It seems only yesterday that Billie Jean King was playing her epic match with Bobby Riggs in the Houston Astrodome. That was the tennis player's version of man's walk on the moon. Since then, tennis has grown into a completely different sport. Racquets are bigger—midsize, over-size and odd-size. Some have curves in the handle. Some are made out of space-age materials. And it isn't only racquets. Tennis shoes display complex engineering—their grip soles literally drink perspiration—and clothing is tight-fitting and comes in various colors. But maybe the biggest change of all has occurred in the area of conditioning, especially in stretching and nutrition. You can talk about the huge prize money, the burgeoning endorsement contracts, and the revolution in equipment, but most dramatic is the difference in training and eating habits.

One of the more delicate problems I face is convincing my students of the importance of good eating. I can correct their forehands, and the results are evident immediately. But with someone who's a little heavy, you have to wait a few months to see that better eating and more exercise can have a positive effect.

Just as some students have more "natural" ability than others, so also are some students more "naturally" fit. Or unfit. One of the failures of my career has been Fritz Buehning. I believe Fritz has as much talent as almost any player I have coached. He is big and strong, with a wonderful power game, but what makes him unique is the remarkable feel and touch he has in his hands. Fritz is a big man with a little guy's reflexes. A great combination.

Nick wants Fritz Buehning to work all the time. Sometimes he does, sometimes he doesn't. . . .

Off the court, however, Fritz has poor eating habits. He's a muncher. He never met a potato chip he didn't enjoy, and like a lot of tennis players he'll quaff a beer or two after a workout. The result is that Fritz has a bit of a spare tire around the middle. It's like a weight belt. He has to lug it around with him all the time. Who knows how much it hurts him? Definitely, it doesn't help.

Ann Quinn, a nutritionist and physical therapist on the staff at the Academy, wasn't around years ago when Fritz was coming up through the program. We were a smaller group then, and the science of physiology was not the well-researched and extensive agenda it is now. Nobody really paid much attention to such things as diet, stretching, and weight training. Now all three are each as much a part of our program as the on-court instruction. Each of our students is given a guide for a balanced diet that includes the four basic food groups. A deficiency in any one can mean trouble on the court.

At the back of the book is an appendix of questions and answers on nutrition by Ann Quinn where you'll find a lot of information. Here we'll just cite the main food groups:

Milk and Milk Products. This group includes milk, cheese, yogurt. These foods contain an abundance of minerals such as calcium and of vitamins B-2, B-12, and A.

Bread, Cereals, Rice and Spaghetti. These are strong in carbohydrates, vitamin E, and the B-complex vitamins.

Citrus Fruits, Tomatoes, Salad Greens. This group includes spinach, turnips, carrots, pumpkins, and squash. They are all excellent sources of vitamin A, vitamin E, and the B-group vitamins, plus minerals.

Potatoes and Other Fruits and Vegetables. Potatoes, broccoli, green peppers, and cauliflower are important vegetables in this group; high-nutrition fruits include berries, cherries, melons, and peaches. All provide vitamin C, minerals, and protein.

You'll notice that no allowance is made for junk foods such as potato chips or cookies. I believe, and Ann Quinn concurs, that tennis players who exercise on a regular basis will have no problem with weight if they DO NOT eat candy and junk food snacks. This stuff contains nothing but sugar and fats high in calories.

There is no excuse for a tennis player to be overweight. Considering the amount of extra training we do at the

Academy, it's almost impossible for our students to be heavy unless they are eating *way* too much. I'll always remember a model I once knew, a really thin girl who seemed to eat sensibly. One day at lunch she was discussing a popular diet plan that was in vogue at the time. "I don't know how people do it," she said. "It's a really *hard* diet. I don't know how people can force themselves to eat that *much* food." If you look at most so-called diet plans, they make allowances for three full meals a day, plus snacks, plus desserts. And even then people cheat with candy and junk foods. And they wonder why they don't lose weight. The best rule is to eat until you are not quite full, and drink a lot of water.

At the Academy we have a "Weight Watcher's Club." It is a voluntary plan. Just as we want players to manage themselves on the court, we also want them to take control of their lives off the court. This is a difficult lesson for many youngsters. Often, they come to us just as they are going through adolescence, when their energy quotients are high and their self-discipline low. Their parents have indulged them all their lives. They come from well-to-do, affluent environments where it's almost a badge of success not to deprive yourself of anything. At the Academy, everyone in our dieters' club aims to lose two pounds per week, or the equivalent of 7000 calories. No one cuts out meals. They *cut down* on their meals. They do a little more exercise. Absolutely taboo, however, are those donuts, snack machine goodies, soft drinks, and so forth. No way they're going to find those around the Academy.

I'll always remember what Paul Dudley White, who was President Dwight Eisenhower's physician, once told the former chief executive: "If you want to know how flabby your brain is, feel your leg muscles." Well, the flabby leg muscles are long gone from professional tennis. Years ago you had the Aussies—the fun-loving Australians who treated tennis as a prelude to drinking beer. Then came the disco kings, a bunch of guys who were on the leading edge of the big money explosion in the seventies and who spent it while gliding along in the fast lane. Now there's a new breed. The veterans on the tour look at these kids coming up and call them the Robots. These young guys and gals are serious. They train, train, train. Then for dessert they do calisthenics. Nautilus is the vitamin bottle of the eighties.

I call it Power Tennis. When Jimmy Arias hits his forehand, you need good vision just to *see* the ball, much less return it.

And standing up to Chip Hooper's serve is a formidable task in itself. Chip doesn't break racquets, he melts them.

At our Academy we have a full complement of Nautilus machines. Only a few years ago, weight lifting was deemed counterproductive to tennis. It would "shorten" your muscles, purists said. Well, even tennis dogma can change. I say this: If weight training tightens you up, what's to prevent you from doing stretching exercises to loosen you up? Build your strength with resistance work. Run, run, run. And keep your flexibility with stretching.

Children cannot foresee the benefits of stretching. When you are young, you can run all day, and you never feel stiff in the evening. But in your twenties, you begin to notice the tightness. Then it is more difficult to stretch out those hamstrings. I say make stretching a part of your daily regimen from the beginning. On pages 62-66, you'll find a step-by-step stretching program developed by the Academy's Ann Quinn. Our students use it every day, and so can you. Develop good habits. Keep your flexibility. Compare your body to an engine. A flexible body is a well-oiled engine. A tight body has to work that much harder. It's less efficient.

Children today quickly pick up the rudimentary parts of the sport. They may find it harder to concentrate on their off-court training. But that is just where they can make a big breakthrough.

People look for excuses. When Jimmy Arias goes to Japan, the Japanese press often asks him, "How come the Japanese players are not so good? Is it because they're small?" Arias is small, but he has pushed and trained himself to play a big man's game. He has made himself bigger. When he first began his pro career, somewhat mysteriously he started having muscle cramps during matches. It took us awhile to figure it out. He was competing at a more furious pace. He was pumped up. His body, shot full of adrenaline, carried him to the point of exhaustion, but in the course of concentrating and playing so hard, Jimmy didn't feel the fatigue. The consequence was muscle cramping. He had to do a little more work off the court. He began running more, upping his mileage to some three miles a day.

Torben Ulrich, the long-time champion from Denmark, still plays the Grand Masters circuit at age 56. He is in phenomenal condition. Women sigh at the shape of his leg muscles. Torben often goes on long training runs, and he carries a jump rope in his equipment bag. Jumping rope is great, especially if you're in a place where jogging a few miles is not possible or recommended.

A decade ago it was considered a feat to be able to complete a marathon. Now we have the Ironman Competition, in which the athletes swim almost 2½ miles in the ocean, bicycle some 122 miles, and then, hardly pausing to catch their breath, go out and run a marathon.

It is a natural process to run. Back at the beginning of time, prehistoric man probably ran to catch his quarry, to put food on the kitchen table in his cave. I'm on top of my students all of the time: "Did you do your running?" "Did you do your stretching?" "Have you done your Nautilus work?" These are habits that must be part of your routine, as much as the work on your groundstrokes and your serve. Once you are in shape, it's easy to stay there. But first you must push yourself past those barriers of pain, past those points of tedium where the reward seems too distant and remote to make any sense.

Aaron Krickstein has won 44 straight junior matches and five consecutive junior national championships. He's done most of it through tremendous ability. But recently Aaron has been enjoying his success. He's been working—in fact, working hard by most standards—but no way has he worked hard enough for me. He's lost matches he should not have lost. Well, Aaron and I are headed for a showdown. Sometime soon, maybe after he loses another match in which he can't get to an important drop shot, or he starts to get tired and he lets down on the big points, then I'll go to him and tell him, "Aaron, the party's over. Now it's time to work. Get your butt out there and run. Do the Nautilus. Do your stretching. Watch your diet." Only I probably won't be that genteel. I want Aaron Krickstein to have the attitude of Jimmy Arias. I want him to be a fighter.

George Allen, the legendary pro football coach, is headed for the Hall of Fame because of his ability to take retreads, castoffs, and players no one else wanted, and mold them into a winning team. Allen does some physical exercise every day, and his philosophy is this: "Always do one more than you want to do." That means set your goals, and then exceed them. You do that on and off the court, and, hey, the rest is easy.

Fitness is the key to the mental approach to the game. Check your leg to see if your brain is flabby. Watch the world's top players. Apart from their skill and technique, notice their court speed, their agility, how they stretch and retrieve and still maintain a balanced position. Appreciate their endurance and strength. These are qualities you must strive to emulate.

Once a father contacted me to ask if his son was too young, at 18 months of age, to begin a jogging program. I thought that was taking a good thing a little too far. He should wait at least until the boy is two years old. Seriously, it's difficult to say what is the earliest age to begin such a program. Stretching can be done from square one even before a child has learned to walk. And while physiologists have tried to determine if jogging at a young age can have detrimental effects over the long haul, there seems to be no concrete evidence to suggest it does. I say watch young children at play. It seems to me that they are running constantly, anyway. It's just that they break it up with short rests.

There are three main physical goals to strive for with your off-court conditioning: endurance, flexibility, and strength. Luckily, we can thank the Japanese for giving us the greatest invention in history to help you accomplish these goals: the Walkman stereo cassette player. As the bumper sticker says, "Do it to music." Listening to your favorite sounds can alleviate the boredom of conditioning. The Walkman for kids is like the mirror for body builders. The muscle guys exercise in front of a mirror and watch their pectorals expand. A kid can do 100 situps while listening to rock and roll.

Cardiovascular endurance—the capacity of the heart and lungs to supply oxygen to the brain—was until recently rarely considered in terms of a physical fitness program for tennis students. The prevailing wisdom was that tennis in itself was a conditioning tool: play more tennis, get more fit. But now scientists have discovered that tennis is *not* the most efficient means of conditioning. In fact, several other sports are superior. The stop-start aspect of tennis is similar to kids at play— you get your rest. For endurance, you need long, easy runs, 20 to 30 minutes each, three to four times a week. At a minimum. Also mix in some speed work, alternating the slow pace with some sustained bursts of running at a quick clip just short of a sprint. It's a great way to build up your condition so that you won't get winded when you play a long point that involves a lot of side-to-side and up-and-back running.

I also recommend doing interval work, in which you run real sprints for short distances and take a bit of recovery time after each. Quick, quick, quick. Your feet will fly after a few months of this.

STRETCHING EXERCISES FOR TENNIS FLEXIBILITY

1. Neck Circles. Standing in an upright position, rotate head slowly to the right, touching chin to chest and continuing in a circular motion. Repeat to the other side.

2. Stretching Triceps and Top of Shoulders. With arms overhead, hold the elbow of one arm with the hand of the other arm. Gently pull the elbow behind your head, creating a stretch (photo A). Hold this stretch for 15 seconds. Then, with one arm extended above and the other extended down beside you, push backward with both hands and hold the stretch (photo B) for 15 seconds. Stretch both sides.

3. Arm Rotations. Extend both arms to the sides and rotate, elbows stiff, first forward, then backward.

4. Hip Rotations. Hands on hips, feet slightly spread, rotate hips clockwise, then counterclockwise.

5. Stomach Exercises, Back Curl. Start on your back with knees bent, off the floor, feet interlocked and hands interlaced behind your head at ear level. Curl up, bringing your shoulder blades off the floor about 30°, then lower them back down to the floor (photo C). Make sure to keep your head in a fixed position; bobbing it will strain your neck. When you lower your body, the back of your head should not touch the floor, because you are holding your chin near your chest.

6. Stomach Exercises, Scissors. Lying on your back, with legs extended, scissor up and down, elevating and lowering your legs, but never touching the ground (photo D). Continue for 10 seconds, and then build up further.

7. Stretching the Extensor Muscles of the Back and Hip. Lying face down with arms placed behind head and legs extended, raise right leg and hold for five seconds. Do same

PHOTO A

The Academy stretching program.

PHOTO C

PHOTO B

PHOTO D

with the left leg, then both legs and hold. Finally, elevate head and legs simultaneously and hold the stretch for five to 10 seconds.

8. Stretching the Rotator Muscles of the Lower Back and Pelvic Region. Lie on your back with legs spread and arms extended out at shoulder level (palms up). Cross right leg over left, keeping the left leg on the floor. Make sure to keep your shoulders, arms and back on the floor as the right leg is extended across to the extended opposite hand. Hold for ten seconds. Alternate legs.

9. Stretching the Groin Area. In the sitting position, push the soles of your feet together and gently lean forward, bending from the hips—until you feel the stretch in your groin (photo E). Hold position for 30 seconds. Pushing down with elbows on your legs will increase stability and balance, and thus make it easier to stretch.

10. Stride Stretcher for Lower Back Muscles, Hip Flexers and Leg Muscles. Begin by leaning forward on your hands with your right leg flexed under your chest, and your left leg stretched out behind. With your arms straight and your forward heel on the floor, push your hips down toward floor, keeping leg extended behind (photo F). Hold for 30 seconds. Repeat the exercise with other leg behind.

11. Hamstring Stretch. With legs together in a semituck position and clasping ankles (photo G), stand up so legs are completely extended, still holding onto ankles (photo H). Hold this stretch for 15 seconds.

12. Quadriceps Stretch. Lying outstretched on your stomach, reach behind and grab your left ankle and pull toward your bottom (photo I). Hold this position for 15 seconds and then repeat with the other leg. Next, hold both ankles for 15 seconds (photo J). Then, still in this position, elevate head and shoulders (photo K).

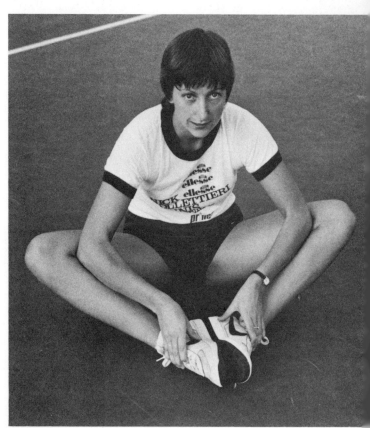

PHOTO E

PHOTO F

PHOTO G

PHOTO H

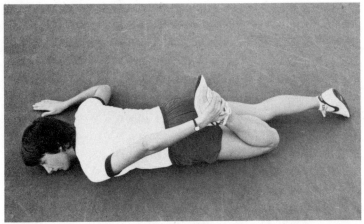

PHOTO I

PHOTO J

PHOTO K

13. Stretching the Calf and Achilles Tendon. Stand facing a wall or fence from a few feet away and lean on it with your forearms. Stand with one leg in front of the other, the front leg bent and the back leg straight behind. Slowly move your hips forward, keeping your lower back flat. Make sure you keep the heel of your straight leg on the ground and hold for 30 seconds. Do not bounce. Stretch other leg.

To stretch the Achilles tendon (and calf), lower your hips downward and bend your knee. Your back should still be flat, your heel down. Hold for 25 seconds. Stretch legs.

14. Stretching Ankles. In a sitting position, elevate leg off the floor and trace the alphabet in the air with the foot. This will ensure that the ankle is moved through its complete range of motion and will both strengthen and stretch its muscles and tendons.

A typical Interval Training program consists of several sets of exercises. In the first set, you might do a series of eight 50-yard dashes, resting for 30 seconds between each. The next set would be composed of fewer repetitions and longer distances, say, six 100-yard sprints, resting for 60 seconds between each. Set three: four 150-yard sprints, resting for 90 seconds between each. Set four: two 200-yard sprints, resting for 120 seconds between each. Set five: four 150-yard sprints, resting for 90 seconds between each. Set six: six 100-yard sprints, resting for 60 seconds between each. Set seven: Eight 50-yard sprints, resting for 30 seconds between each.

In this program, you start with very short, fast distances, build up gradually to longer sprints with longer recovery, and then finish off with the short, quick sprints again. Monitor your heartbeat. Between each set, it is important that your heart rate decline to 120 beats per minute. Between each repetition, your heart beat should recover to 150 beats per minute. (You can time your pulse for 10 seconds, then multiply by six.)

Besides running, I suggest you mix your cardiovascular work with skipping rope, swimming, bike riding, or aerobic dancing. Don't allow monotonous exercise to turn your conditioning program stale.

A player with a high degree of flexibility has excellent range on the court. But this is a two-edged sword. The more you are able to stretch, the greater the danger of injury as you stress your body to reach a shot. Therefore you should not only concentrate on stretching such obvious parts as your hamstrings, but also try to increase your range of motion through all of the joints, including arms and shoulders. Make stretching the *end* punctuation of your daily workouts, and stretch whenever you find an extra minute or two. Keep those muscles flexible.

As for strength, its benefits are obvious. A good big man always will beat a good little man, all else being equal. For years, weight lifting was criticized as a training tool. It would "bunch" muscles. And only five years ago, people still were saying that women could not benefit from weight lifting. The rise in women's body building in that short span has disproved the theory. In any case, I think people should go into physical training with an open mind. See what works for you. Nautilus workouts provide an excellent way to build strength while maintaining flexibility. Weight lifting also builds

The Nick Bollettieri Power Handle: stretching shoulder muscles, back muscles, and the arm muscles as used in serving.

Using the SportStick at the Academy: To develop strength and flexibility through the full range of motion of the tennis stroke, a new device called SportStick is utilized as a warm-up tool prior to practice. Photos illustrate an instructor using resistance drills to warm up the backhand, forehand, and service strokes. The SportStick is also used to stretch the leg, ankle, and shoulder muscles prior to and after strenuous play.

strength. Even calisthenics are helpful. A wonderful device for tennis players, especially those who travel a lot, is my own Nick Bollettieri Power Handle, which allows you to accomplish a variety of exercises. Another device we use is the SportStick, a fabulous tool for stretching and strengthening throughout the full range of motion.

With Nautilus or any other weight-lifting equipment, use lighter weights and more repetitions. You want to work your muscles almost to failure rather than to "max out" with a heavy weight and only two or three repetitions.

Also, strive for an overall program that utilizes all of your muscles: lower body, upper body, and arms. Leg lifts are excellent for building strength in your thighs. Toe raises strengthen your calves. The best exercises for the upper body are the bench press, the military or standing press, and dumbbell presses on an incline bench. Arm work consists of bicep curls and tricep exercises. For a good tricep exercise, get a close grip on the bar, then lift the weights to a resting position behind your head. Press upward for 10 or 12 repetitions.

Despite the tremendous changes that have occurred in tennis over recent years, in everything from equipment to training methods, in one respect "remembering the old days" can be very helpful. I maintain that you should keep a training diary. A lot of top runners do it, including Alberto Salazar and Bill Rogers. They record in detail every bit of physical activity, as well as what food they eat and the amount of sleep they get each night. The benefits are obvious. If you suffer an injury, or feel fatigued, the diary may well give you a clue as to why.

A tennis training program should be structured under certain conditions. Make it specific—that is, relate your training to tennis, both as to the muscle groups involved and as to the energy sources you build.

Don't be afraid of overloading. No pain, no gain. Remember that stress is the catalyst behind improvement. Try also to fit your program to yourself. Just because someone else does a certain exercise doesn't mean that you would benefit by doing it. Gauge your needs and goals and work toward them. And finally, have fun. Hard work need not be the stuff of salt mines. Convince yourself of the benefits of training, and you will enjoy it.

Nautilus conditioning: working on legs, arms, and upper body.

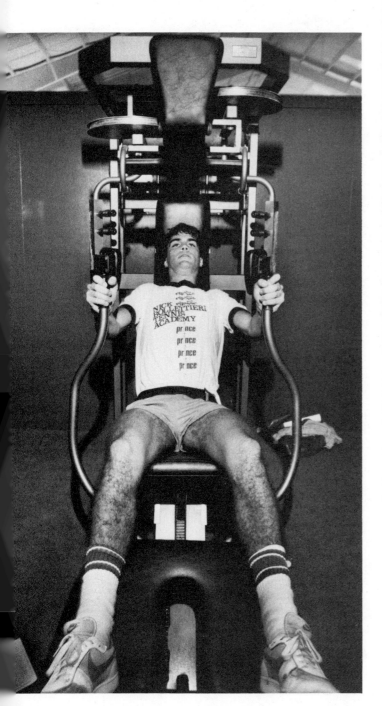

6

BASIC TENNIS

People always ask me if I have any secrets to success. There aren't any secrets, I tell them. I don't know of any. What I do know is how to motivate people, how to get them to work. I can look at someone and see their weaknesses. I can look at their opponents and figure out a plan to attack them. But secrets? As Brian Gottfried says, "The secret is to work hard."

I try to change attitudes, not strokes. But don't get me wrong. I know my tennis. If I see a kid making a mistake, I'm all over him. "Get the racquet head out in front." "Low to high." "Finish over your shoulder." I go home at night and my voice is hoarse from yelling. I'm like a poker player who has just finished a 10-hour session. Poker players lie in bed and see cards. I lie in bed and see forehands.

The important thing is not to waste time. In junior tennis, the race is a sprint. Don't give the other kids a head start by picking up the game without proper instruction. Get the basics early. Learn the fundamentals. If you don't build on a solid base, and if you have flaws, eventually your game comes tumbling down.

Here are some tips to get you started. We're going to go long on pictures and short on words, because I believe that seeing is the best way to learn. And you're going to get some actual lessons, just like the ones I give my own students. I expect this chapter to be well used over the years. I want you to wear out its pages, reading them over and over. But even more, I want you to wear out your racquets and shoes on the practice court. I want to see the soles of your shoes rubbed clean. I want to see racquet grips worn smooth. We're going to give you the basics of instruction. It's up to you to make them into your secrets of success. How? Only one way: with work.

Picking a Racquet

Once, big heavy racquets with large grips were the staple of tournament players. Now, lighter racquets with smaller grips and large hitting areas are the rule. Experiment with different racquets to find the one that suits you. Keep in mind that the old standard-size wood racquet is quickly becoming obsolete. Every player in the world has been beaten by someone using one of the "flyswatters," the somewhat derogatory name given to the oversize 110 racquets when they were first introduced. It's interesting to note, also, that while many players are switching to the larger racquets, traffic the other way—from oversize 110 to standard—is almost nonexistent. In any case, by now there are so many models to choose from, it would be foolish of me to try to specify one type or another that will be just right for you. Go to a good pro shop and check them out. You'll *feel* the right one for you.

The Grip

Probably one of the more interesting changes in teaching in recent years is the encouragement of a varied style. It used to be that players were taught one grip, and they stuck to it. Now, I think it is important that you learn *all* the grips. Each has its benefits. Each has its limitations. Certain grips are suited to high balls. Certain ones are better for low balls and approach shots. Learn their characteristics *early*. You must be flexible—versatile enough to adapt to any situation.

With the grip, you're trying to produce a vertical racquet head at impact. This is an absolute must. To achieve this position, you'll have to experiment until you discover what's best for *you*. But no matter which grip you use, keep in mind that your hand position is constant throughout the stroke. Once you choose your grip and begin the stroke, stick with it.

The grips include the following.

Eastern Forehand: This is a fairly simple grip and quite easy to master. To achieve the Eastern grip, place your palm on the backside of the racquet, then pretend you are shaking hands with the racquet. Hold the palm of the hand and the racquet handle vertical at all times. Two hints: Having gripped the racquet handle, spread apart your fingers slightly for better

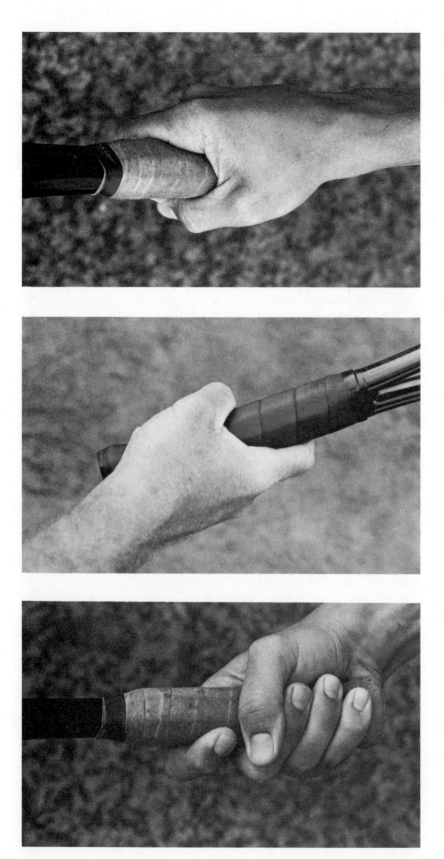

Forehand grips:
Eastern,
Semi-Western,
and Western.

strength and control. And the thumb should settle between the first and second fingers and around the handle.

Semi-Western Forehand: This grip gives added strength by placing the palm more to the right side of the racquet handle, thereby putting the hand behind the ball at impact. To achieve the Semi-Western position, grip in an Eastern style, then move your hand about a quarter-turn to the right. Ivan Lendl, Jimmy Arias, and Jose-Luis Clerc use this grip in their modern Power Game. Of all the grips, I feel that the Semi-Western is the best and offers a player the best chance to develop a real "weapon."

Western Forehand: This grip can produce exaggerated top-spin, especially on high balls, but it is less effective on the low, skidding ball, the type normally seen on grass surfaces. Harold Solomon uses the Western forehand because he rarely plays on grass. To achieve the Western position, move your hand another quarter-turn to the right from the Semi-Western forehand. Now the palm is almost under the racquet handle.

Eastern Backhand: For this grip, hold the throat of your racquet with your nonhitting hand. Grip the racquet in the Eastern forehand position. Now move your hand a quarter-turn to the left. This grip is extremely effective for approach shots, drop shots, chip service returns, and slices.

Semi-Western Backhand: Because of its topspin production, this grip is favored by such pros as Jose-Luis Clerc and Ivan Lendl. But be very careful. It's difficult to master. Even Jimmy Arias, as gifted as he is, needed eight solid weeks of practice, hitting thousands and thousands of balls, before he could make the change to a Semi-Western backhand. But once he managed it, his backhand improved enormously. For a Semi-Western grip, establish an Eastern backhand, then move your hand a quarter-turn to the left.

Continental: I call this the "lazy player's grip," which should give you a hint as to what I think of it. The grip gets its name from Europe, where playing on slow surfaces produces a low bounce. It's effective on low balls, but in today's power game, the Continental is seen less and less. The problem is that it tends to break down under pressure. Basically, the Continental is a hybrid, halfway between the Eastern forehand and an

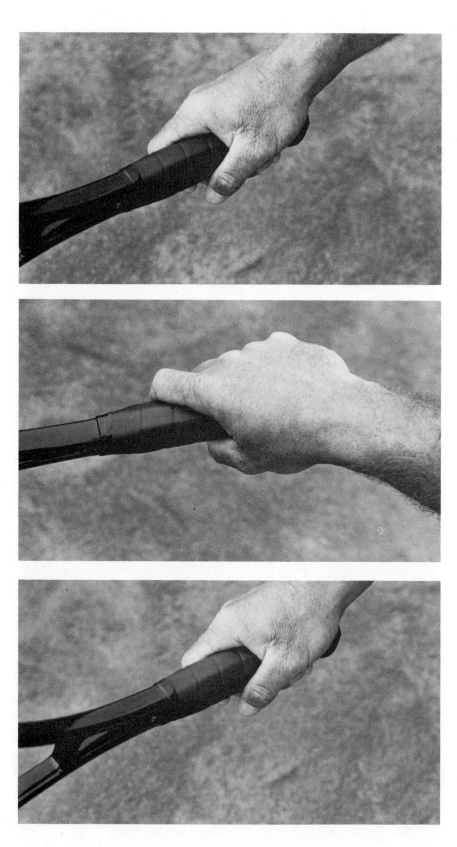

Backhand grips:
Eastern, Western,
and Semi-Western.

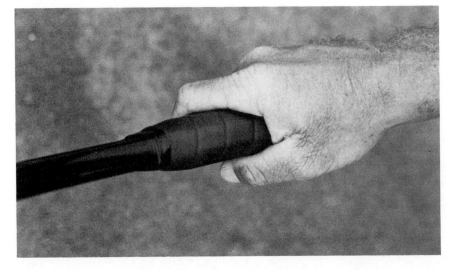

Continental grip.

Eastern backhand. You use the Continental for both strokes (hence, the "lazy player's grip"). To achieve a Continental position, hold the racquet face vertical and take a "hammer grip" on the handle, as if you were going to use the racquet edge to pound a nail.

Ready Position

This area does not receive nearly enough attention. Develop good fundamentals here and you will not have to break bad habits later. A good ready position allows you to make a quick first step and to get your swing moving with the least amount of effort.

The key points:

1. Concentrate on the ball at all times.
2. Be relaxed. If you tighten up, your reaction time increases.
3. Keep your nonhitting hand on the throat of the racquet to help you make grip changes.
4. Keep moving forward. This forces you to hit the ball out in front.
5. Keep your feet at shoulder width. Keep your arms and racquet slightly away from your body, to allow you to turn better.
6. Maintain a positive frame of mind. Think "I will," rather than "I may not be able to."

The ready position:
Geoffrey Marks,
Carling Bassett (two hands),
and Mike DePalmer.
Everybody has a different style.

The Forehand

Everyone hits the forehand with slight variations. The style that feels comfortable is the best for you. However, certain basics are essential to this shot. These include:

1. A good ready position.
2. Taking the racquet head back quickly.
3. Smooth release of the entire stroke.
4. Hitting from low to high with a long, extended follow-through.

The success of the stroke is assured on the backswing, and interestingly enough, it is here that the greatest variety is shown. It almost seems as if everyone's backswing is slightly different, like fingerprints. Some people take the racquet back with the head held high. Others take it back with the head at waist level or below. It is important, however, that at the end of the backswing, the racquet be positioned *below* the level of the ball, which allows you to hit up and through for power, control and topspin.

STRAIGHT-BACK FOREHAND

Here are the important elements of the *straight-back* forehand:

1. From the ready position, racquet is pulled straight back without dropping or raising the head.
2. Racquet head goes back first.
3. Backswing is compact, with racquet head pointing at the back fence at completion of backswing.
4. Beginning the forward swing, allow the racquet to go below the ball.
5. Follow-through is high. Keep the arm relaxed.
6. Shoulders are rotated going back and opened up naturally coming through the shot. Do not force the shoulders or try to push the ball with physical strength.
7. Keep your follow-through long and relaxed at all times, letting the racquet head do its work.

NICK:

Chris, I think your backswing is starting to smooth out. It seems as if the extra motions and jerks you had are almost gone. This will help your forehand quite a bit.

CHRIS:

I keep trying to get my racquet back quickly, but even so there are times when under pressure I am late meeting the ball out in front.

NICK:

Try this. Stand in the ready position. Now make sure your racquet head goes back first. The mistake you have been making is that you have been starting the backswing with your elbow. You wind up dragging the racquet back, and at some point in the swing you must make a correction or else hit the ball late. It is simpler to think of the racquet head going back first.

CHRIS:

I can see what a difference that makes. Now I am able to handle the hard forcing shots.

Brad Gilbert and the straight-back forehand: racquet back, shoulders turned, step, hit through ball, finish.

LOOP FOREHAND

Here are the elements of the *loop* forehand:

1. Nonhitting hand pushes up the racquet head as soon as possible.
2. The backswing and forward swing are continuous.
3. Keep the loop compact.
4. Follow through in a natural motion. Let the racquet head go out to the target or even back around your shoulder, whichever feels more natural.

NICK:

Jimmy, you have a super forehand, but even so, it can be better. You've picked up a couple of flaws in your backswing that are making it difficult for you to hit shots that are deep and fast. Stand inside the baseline now while I volley at your feet. This will make you start your backswing quickly in order to hit returns.

Aaron Krickstein and the loop forehand: preparation, racquet high, racquet head below ball, hitting through, finish.

JIMMY:
You're right. I can't seem to get through the ball.

NICK:
Your backswing is the problem. Your "loop" is too pronounced when you take back the racquet. You need to start sooner and to cut the loop in half, to give yourself more time.

JIMMY:
That's better. I'm hitting the ball low-to-high very easily now.

NICK:
You've gotten rid of that wasted motion. The secret is to start your loop backswing by pushing the racquet head up with your nonhitting hand. But don't get it up too high. You want to keep your swing compact. I like your follow-through. Your elbow is moving away from your body on the forward part of your swing. This produces a nice relaxed stroke and the "hitting out" feeling we want you to strive for. I love the way you open up your hips through the stroke and the way you accelerate your racquet head on contact. Your dad always insisted on that relaxed motion and it's the best I've ever seen.

The Backhand

Many players have a fear of the backhand, usually because they develop the forehand first. For a good player, however, the backhand produces no trepidation. Actually, it is the more natural stroke, and ultimately the easier to master.

All of the elements of the backhand are the same.

1. Bring the racquet head back quickly, utilizing the non-hitting hand.
2. Keep the swing smooth.
3. Watch the ball.
4. Hit low-to-high.

To improve a weak one-hand backhand, first look to your grip. I feel that you need at least an Eastern backhand grip, because you're hitting from the weaker side physically. You can offset this by making a quick shoulder turn and being sure that the racquet head leads the backswing. In addition, maintain a firm wrist, meet the ball in front, and be certain you follow through completely. Let the racquet head "go" on the follow-through. Watch how relaxed players like Jimmy Arias seem to be as they complete the follow-through, the racquet whipping up and over the ball. Once again, you're striving for a low-to-high swing.

Jimmy Arias and the one-hand backhand: early preparation, turn, racquet back, follow-through (head still).

NICK:
Danielle, today we're going to concentrate on your backhand. It's good, but not as solid as I would like. You're making a couple of small errors that are hurting you.

DANI:
I've noticed that the ball seems to get behind me when I run wide for a backhand.

NICK:
Your first move on the backhand must be to turn your shoulder. This gets the racquet head back quickly. You're also making a footwork error. When you reach the ball, make sure you are stepping toward the net, not sideways. Step sideways and you "jam" yourself. Step to the ball. Now watch how much harder you hit the ball. One final thing—you do something that I call a "double backswing." You get the racquet back fine, and then, just as you are about to make your forward swing, you take it back farther. This was a little quirk that Bjorn Borg had. But Dani, I don't think you and Borg have the same timing. To eliminate those late hits, you must take it back and then forward in one motion.

DANI:
You keep saying how important the backswing is. How about mine?

NICK:
Except for that occasional ''double backswing,'' it's fine. Your nonhitting hand pulls the racquet head straight back with your arm fairly close to your body. You have a slight loop. Some people take the racquet straight back, others loop it like you do. The important thing is to get the racquet head below the ball as you begin your forward swing.

DANI:
Sometimes I overrun balls.

NICK:
It's better to reach for the ball. This helps you swing up and out. Once again, we call this ''hitting out.'' It makes your swing fluid and relaxed. Also, once you start your swing, don't slow down. This ensures a nice and long follow-through.

DANI:

Sometimes I think I ought to switch to a two-hander to try to get more power.

NICK:

You can get all the power you need with the one-hander, and reach more balls, if you get that shoulder turned on the backswing. The more you turn the shoulder, the farther your backswing. This ''winding'' effect is like a spring coiling and uncoiling.

DANI:

Why can't I lay back my wrist and get power that way?

NICK:

It's true that you will be able to swing the racquet faster that way, but you lose control. You must keep the wrist fixed on the backswing. We're going to work a few weeks on the shot. If you don't develop power, we might think about switching to a Semi-Western backhand grip. I think the best thing for you is to practice quickness. Get the shoulder turned. Get the racquet back. Step toward the net.

DANI:

How do I get more topspin?

NICK:

Be sure to get the racquet head under the ball and try to follow through a little higher. That's better. Feel as if at its lowest point you almost brush the ground. You must bend the knees. Now swing low-to-high, brushing the back of the ball and finishing with a nice, high follow-through. That's it. It's simple.

DANI:

What about underspin?

NICK:

Be careful with this shot. Use it only as a change of pace. Now is the time to work on topspin, or the flat backhand. If you hit a slice, or underspin backhand, all the time, you will find your opponents attacking. However, slice can be used to throw off an opponent's timing, and it's especially effective off low balls. Instead of dropping the racquet head on the backswing, keep it elevated above the ball. On the forward part of your swing, hit down and out, brushing the back of the ball.

DANI:

Why didn't you start me with an underspin backhand?

NICK:

That's a defensive shot, as I've said. Yet it's important. You will find this is the shot you use when you approach the net, because it gives you *more time to close in. Also, the spin produces a low-bouncing ball that your opponent will have trouble with.*

DANI:
Do I have to change my backswing or the face of the racquet, or use my wrist to develop this shot? I've noticed that with some players, like John McEnroe, it looks as if the racquet face is parallel to the ground when they contact the ball.

NICK:
That's not true. It only looks that way. Just before hitting the ball, every player has the racquet face almost vertical to the ground. They brush down the lower back of the ball, then finish up and out. The wrist stays very firm. For all your shots, try to keep your racquet face on the backswing the same—slightly open. This will make your opponent guess a split second longer as to what type of backhand you are hitting.

One more point—the underspin can also be used as a change of pace against a big hitter or as a way to give you time to get back to position after returning a particularly wide, deep, or low ball.

The Two-Hander: It is difficult to say whether the one-hand or the two-hand backhand is better. Some claim the one-hander gives you more reach. Others say the two-hander is more reliable, and easier for children to learn.

To complicate matters further, there are several variations of the two-hand backhand. One is the *guide backhand*. In this one, the player finishes with the racquet and arms pointing where he or she wants the ball to go. With the *wraparound backhand*, the arms continue on and wrap around the shoulders. This stroke normally has more wrist acceleration, and if hit from low to high, it generates excessive topspin.

There are two basic grips for a two-hander. In the first, both hands are in an Eastern forehand grip. In the second, the bottom hand is positioned anywhere from a Continental to an Eastern backhand grip, and the top hand is in an Eastern forehand grip. This is a more versatile style, since it allows the student to follow through with one hand on wide or short balls and on volleys at the net.

Whichever grip you use, the backswing should have your arms and racquet fairly close to your body at waist level. On the forward part of the swing, the racquet head will drop below the ball, swinging up and out, resulting in heavy topspin.

Lisa Bonder and the two-hand wraparound: early preparation, step, contact, follow-through, finish.

Two-Hand Backhand, One-Hand Release: This stroke could be the backhand of the future. It offers the strength of the two-handed backhand, but also gives you an option to let go on balls that feel unnatural or cause problems because of reach. At the same time, you have the flexibility to utilize the one-handed drop shot, the underslice approach, or a one-handed backhand volley.

Amy Schwartz and the two-hand backhand/one-hand release: good preparation, step, contact, release, finish.

The Volley

This is the only stroke for which I favor the Continental grip, because with it the player does not have to adjust during quick exchanges at the net. Still, some players may find that they need the Eastern forehand and backhand grips, to get more strength on their shots.

There are certain key elements to the volley:

1. Get into a good ready position. Be alert, like a goal-tender watching the puck.

2. Relax your knees. Keep your racquet in front of you, holding your elbows well away from your body. The non-hitting hand must rest lightly on the throat if you utilize the one-handed volley, or be placed next to the bottom hand if you are a two-handed volleyer.

3. Block the ball. Get the feeling that you are "catching" it on your racquet. Strive for a very short backswing and follow-through. Later, with experience, you will be able to lengthen your stroke slightly for more power.

4. Always meet the ball in front with your body weight moving forward, into the shot, and maintaining a firm wrist at all times.

Tim Mayotte and the volley. Forehand: ready, turn, short backswing, compact follow-through. Backhand: preparation, short backswing, contact out front, compact finish.

Pam Casale's swing forehand volley.
Carling Bassett's swing backhand volley.

The Serve

I teach three kinds of serve: flat, slice, and spin. You should practice and perfect all three in order to keep your opponent off balance. And remember: the old saying "You are only as good as your second serve" still holds true; develop a consistent deep spin serve that you can control when the pressure is one.

The basic elements of any serve are the same:
1. Position your feet comfortably.
2. Hold the ball lightly in your fingers for the toss.
3. Utilize a minimum of body motion.
4. Develop a fluid, continuous motion.
5. Work on complete extension on contact, getting "the legs" into the serve as well.
6. Finish the stroke completely.

The Flat Serve: The correct grip for this serve is anywhere between the Continental and Eastern backhand grip. Position your feet and distribute your weight comfortably and begin with the ball and racquet out front. With a minimum of body motion, bring the arms down together and up together. The toss should be up and out just slightly to the right of your left foot (if right-handed). Hit the "back of the ball" while reaching up and out with complete extension. You must have good wrist acceleration and make sure you have a smooth full follow-through on the left side of the body.

The Slice: The motion for the slice is the same as that for the flat serve, except that you brush across the right side of the ball, rather than hitting it flat. Be sure to hit up and out. Do not pull down for the slice. Also, you may want to use more of a backhand grip to be able to generate more action on the slice serve. Finally, make sure the entire motion is smooth, accelerating on contact, with a full, relaxed finish.

The Spin: This serve also requires more of a backhand grip. The toss should be a bit farther back and slightly to the left in order for you to brush up the back of the ball on contact. This will produce heavy topspin and results in the high kicking bounce of the spin serve.

Contact:
Flat serve,
slice,
spin.

Eric Korita's 140-mph serve, front and back: preparation, ball toss, reach up, elbow up (front view), extension (back view), follow-through.

The Overhead

The overhead is a serve without the ball toss. It is important to hit up and out, just as you do when serving. Keep this stroke simple and smooth and it will produce many winners. If you try to muscle the ball, you will be asking for trouble.

Essentials of the overhead:

1. Move your feet to get into position.
2. Your nonhitting hand and your racquet go up at the same time. Point to the ball with your free hand. This allows you to concentrate, and to position your shoulders correctly. It also cuts down your backswing and encourages you to hit up and out.
3. Reach up for the ball.
4. Minimize upper body movement.
5. Keep your head up throughout the swing. If the upper part of the body pulls down, you will hit the ball either too shallow or into the net.
6. Use a Continental or Eastern backhand grip. Develop consistency and depth.
7. Confidence is essential. You build confidence through repetition. Once again, you can practice by yourself. Take a ball and hit straight up into the air. Let it bounce on the court, then hit an overhead. Practice, practice, practice.

NICK:
Steve, why do you tell me you can't hit overheads?

STEVE:
I can't seem to judge the ball.

NICK:
Your first move must be to turn sideways. Get your nonhitting hand up into the air, and your racquet head up behind your head. That's it! Now reach for the ball the way you would on a serve. Keep it simple and compact. The overhead is just your service motion slightly abbreviated. Don't try to muscle the ball. And keep that chin up in the air so you don't pull down. Hit through the ball.

STEVE:
I still have a little trouble judging the ball.

NICK:
When in doubt, move back an extra step. It's easier to come in than to backpedal at the last moment. After hitting the overhead, move forward into the net very quickly to be in position to put away the short defensive return forced by your offensive overhead.

Mike DePalmer's overhead smash: good preparation with both arms up, point to the ball, extension and contact, full finish.

The Lob

The lob might be considered the forgotten stepchild of the fundamental strokes—what used to be regarded as a "sissy" shot. Even today people do not pay much attention to it. But it's a shot that you can practice, learn well, and use as a weapon to turn a defensive position into an offensive opportunity.

In days past, the lob was always used only as a last resort—the stroke you hit when you were out of position and needed time to recover. The high defensive lob forces your opponent back and provides you with this necessary time. Times have changed and there are now numerous players who can devastate you with the offensive lob.

Jimmy Connors with his two-handed backhand winds up as if to hit a passing shot and then often glides the ball up and slightly over his opponent's outstretched arm and racket.

Aaron Krickstein has still another lob, the offensive topspin lob hit off both sides with a tremendous amount of overspin.

You must make your opponent at the net feel you are going to try a passing shot. Then, at the last moment, you hit the lob with the same type of preparation and motion as the normal backswing. If you have a good command of this shot, you can really keep your opponent wondering whether you are going to be hitting lobs or passing shots.

A good tip in hitting the topspin lob is to think of the "moonball," the stroke that young players often use from the baseline. This is quite similar to the offensive lob. Aim 10 to 15 feet above the net, hit low-to-high like Connors, or with excessive topspin like Krickstein (brushing quickly up the back of the ball) and enjoy the surprised look on your opponent's face as the ball floats (or spins) over his head for a winner.

Footwork

Coming to a complete stop, turning totally sideways, stepping in with the famous "crossover" step, etc., all used to be rigid requirements in tennis instruction. I do not necessarily disagree with the importance of these points, but I do feel that the greatest emphasis should be placed elsewhere. Above all else, get to every ball! Do not be so concerned with looking pretty and stepping with this foot at this angle or this degree. Simply run to every ball, get set up, and then step in the direction you are hitting the ball. There will be times you will be off-balance, falling backward while hitting, etc. Do not panic. Just make sure you finish the stroke.

And here is another pointer. When Bjorn Borg and Brian Gottfried practice, they run for *every* ball. Notice I said *run,* not shuffle. They are like dogs chasing the rabbit at the race track. Getting to the ball early erases 99 percent of your groundstroke problems. It is a matter of getting all three—racquet, body and feet—moving to the ball like clockwork.

Now you have the basics of tennis, along with good feet, good hands, a big heart, and a lot of guts. But, I am not going to just leave you here. Starting with Chapter 8, we're going to take up the development of a junior player over the span of eight to ten years, and along the way you'll get important variations, refinements, and applications of these basics. You'll still want to come back to this chapter, because this is where it all is. And remember: There is no secret to being a winner. You can be a winner just as easily as anyone else can, as long as you work at it. Practice, develop your style, and stick to it.

7

THE DRILLS

Drills are the backbone of our operation. I know that's like saying paper clips have made IBM great. People snicker when I tell them about the drills and how we spend several hours each day running the kids through fundamental exercises, sometimes with as many as six or eight students on the court. That's where we get the "factory" or "boot camp" label. But even our best players, such as Jimmy Arias and Aaron Krickstein, do the drills, and they believe in them as much as I do.

Look at pro football and baseball teams. What do they do during their training time? Drills. Lots of them. You see photos of pro football players running through agility courses. In spring training, baseball managers stress fundamental plays. Drills are wonderful because they equalize the conditions for everyone. And once all things are equal, it is easy to see the talent, and simple to judge the deficiencies and strengths.

Backhand drill from the baseline.

Après-drill: the ball patrol.

At the Academy, we try to provide an environment of competition and to give the players the facilities and instruction. Drills create a competitive atmosphere in that they duplicate crucial match situations. And you build muscle memory through hitting thousands of balls, so that when you're playing a tournament, your subconscious takes over and produces the result that you worked for months, maybe years, before.

Most people don't know how to practice. They go out and hit a few balls. They should take a cue from the academic world. In law school, there are study groups where students work together to progress. Try to accomplish the same thing in your tennis. Create a drill group, and at least once a week get together and work as a unit. You'll be amazed at how this will help your progress.

In this chapter, you will find all of the drills we use. Some are for groups as large as eight or ten players. Others are suitable for three or four players. Pay strict attention to the latter, because these are the more competitive drills, the ones that put the most pressure on you.

There are seven types of drills: 1–4, for basic groundstrokes; 5–8, for combination groundstrokes; 9–15, for volleys; 16–19, for groundstroke and volley combinations; 20–22, for overheads; 23, for the basic serve; and 24–36, our advanced drills.

NOTE: Be sure to exercise the proper safety procedures when drilling and make sure all balls into the net are cleared immediately.

BASIC GROUNDSTROKE DRILLS

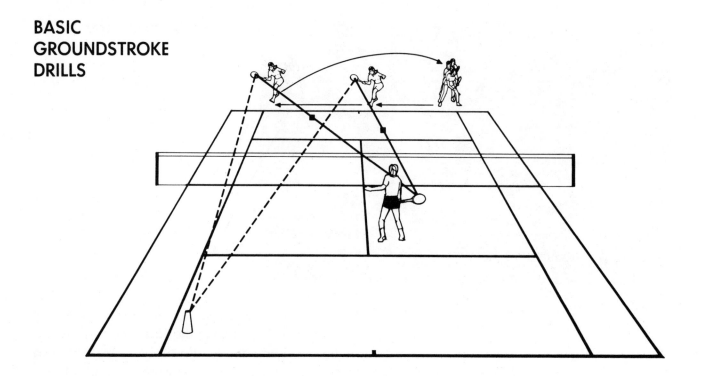

DRILL ONE:
Two balls across baseline.
OBJECTIVES:
To work on the mechanics of the stroke.
To improve control.
To improve consistency.

OPERATION

a. Feeder stands at service line.
b. Players stand on baseline.
c. Feeder hits ball deep to center of baseline. After player hits the ball, feeder hits the second ball wide to the same player. After first player has executed both shots he goes back to the starting line, and the second player starts the drill.
d. It is important to keep the students in line, jogging in place.
e. The target should be placed three feet away from sideline and baseline.

ALTERNATIVES

1. The same drill can be done for backhands.
2. Same drill can be done hitting two balls across court.
3. It is also good to alternate: first ball down line, second ball cross court, or vice versa. (With more than eight players, this alternative works very well. The person in front hits down the line and the person behind hits crosscourt, or vice versa.)
4. When there are more than eight players on the court, feed only one ball.

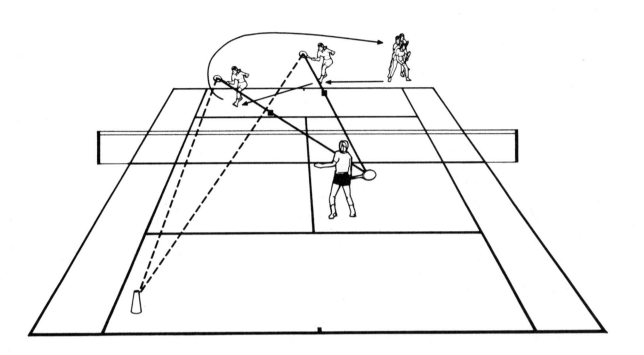

DRILL TWO:
One baseline groundstroke, one approach shot.
OBJECTIVES:
To work on the mechanics of the stroke.
To improve control.
To improve consistency.
To learn to take advantage of short shots.

OPERATION

a. Feeder stands at service line.
b. Players stand on baseline.
c. Feeder hits ball deep to center of baseline; after player hits the ball, feeder hits second ball wide and short (around service line) to the same player. After he has executed both shots, he goes back to the starting line, and the second player starts the drill.
d. Keep everybody moving.
e. During the approach the student should concentrate on a shorter backswing, and should hit down the line (percentage shot).
f. Emphasis should be on making no errors.
g. Target should be three feet from sideline and baseline.

ALTERNATIVES

1. Same drill for backhands.
2. Same drill, alternating placement. First ball crosscourt, second ball down the line.
3. The first ball deep, and on the second ball, student practices the slice approach shot.
4. With more than eight players on the court, feed only one short ball.

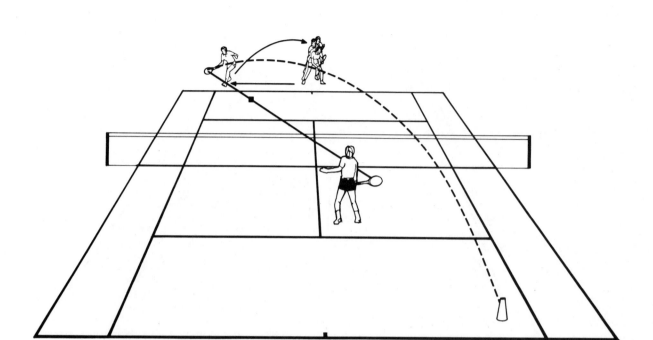

DRILL THREE:
Lobs.
OBJECTIVE:
To develop defensive and offensive lobs.

OPERATION

a. Feeder stands at service line.
b. Players stand on the center of baseline.
c. Feeder hits ball wide and deep. Player must hit the ball over the fully extended arm and racquet of the feeder, into the target area. After hitting the ball, player goes back to the starting line, and second player hits the lob.
d. The offensive topspin lob should be practiced only by advanced players.
e. Keep the rest of students jogging in place.
f. Target should be placed three feet from sideline and baseline.

ALTERNATIVES

1. Same drill for backhands.
2. Two-ball drills, alternating groundstrokes with lobs or drop shots with lobs.

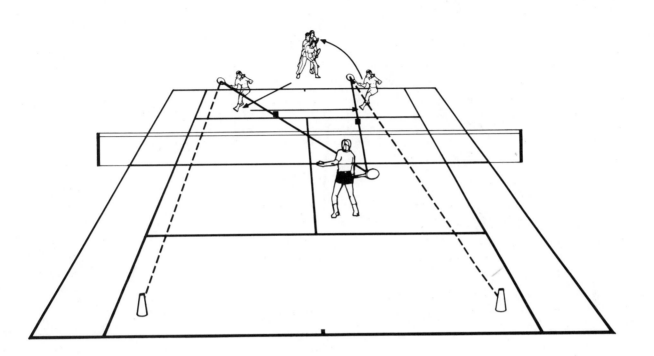

DRILL FOUR:
Forehand weapon development.
OBJECTIVES:
To develop the forehand into a weapon by
forcing student to run around backhand on short
balls.
To make student take advantage of short balls.

OPERATION

a. Feeder stands at service line.
b. Players stand on the center of baseline.
c. The first ball is fed short and high to the
   forehand side, the second ball short and high
   to the backhand.
d. Make sure players are aggressive, but don't
   let them overhit the ball.

ALTERNATIVES

1. Second ball could be inside-out.
2. Let the student run around the backhand for
   the first ball and then follow the shot into the
   net for a volley.
3. When there are more than eight players, let
   the students run around the backhand, hitting
   only one ball.

COMBINATION-GROUNDSTROKES DRILLS

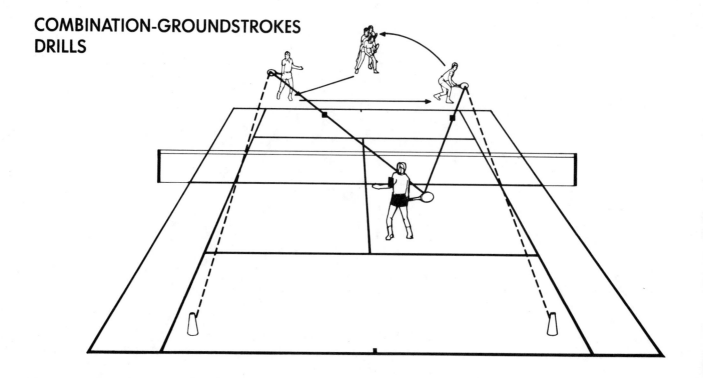

DRILL FIVE:
One forehand, one backhand.
OBJECTIVES:
To work on the mechanics of the stroke.
To improve consistency and control.
To improve footwork.

OPERATION

a. Feeder stands at service line.
b. Players stand on the center of baseline.
c. The first ball is fed wide to the forehand side, the second ball wide to the backhand. After executing both shots, player goes back to the starting line and second player will start drill.
d. Make the players concentrate on form and placement.

ALTERNATIVES

1. Same formation for crosscourts.
2. Alternate first ball down the line, second ball crosscourt, and vice versa.
3. Alternate with drop shots and lobs.
4. When there are more than eight players, use only the one-ball drill. The person in front hits a forehand, the person behind a backhand.
5. After half-a-basket of the original drill, the feeder should hit the ball wide to the backhand and the second ball wide to the forehand.

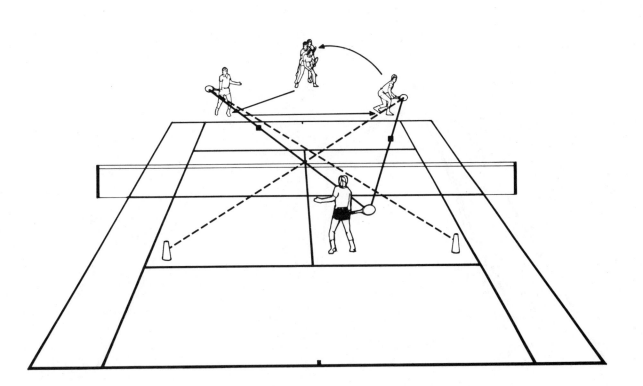

DRILL SIX:
Angle shots.
OBJECTIVES:
To sharpen passing shots.
To work on mechanics of the stroke.
To improve consistency and control.

OPERATION

a. Feeder stands at service line.
b. Players stand on the center of baseline.
c. The first ball is fed wide to the forehand side, the second ball wide to the backhand. After executing both shots, player goes back to starting line and second player goes through the drill.
d. It is important to make the players concentrate on a low-to-high motion.

ALTERNATIVE

1. Alternate first ball down the line, second ball angle shot, and vice versa.

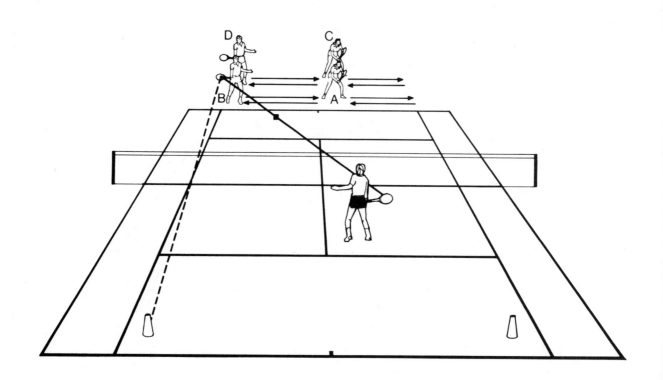

DRILL SEVEN:
Windshield wiper.
OBJECTIVES:
Improve groundstrokes.
Improve consistency and control.
Improve footwork.

OPERATION

a. Instructor stands at service line.
b. Player A stands two feet behind baseline on the singles line, while player B stands two feet behind baseline on the center line.
c. Instructor hits the ball wide to B's right so that he moves over to hit a forehand ground stroke. At the same time, A slides across the center line. When B makes contact with the ball (forehand), instructor hits the ball wide to A's left, forcing him to recover and hit a backhand. As A moves toward his backhand, B is sliding to the center of the court. A and B move as if they are together, hence the "windshield wiper" action.

d. C and D move at the same time A and B move, "shadowing" their groundstrokes. The exercise is repeated until feeder rotates players. Two balls are recommended.

ALTERNATIVES

1. Same pattern for crosscourts.
2. Alternate first ball down line, second ball crosscourt, and vice versa.
3. After A and B hit two shots each, they go to opposite line. So if player A was hitting backhands, the next time around he should be hitting forehands.
4. This drill is also excellent for volleys.
5. First ball groundstroke, second ball drop shot or lob.

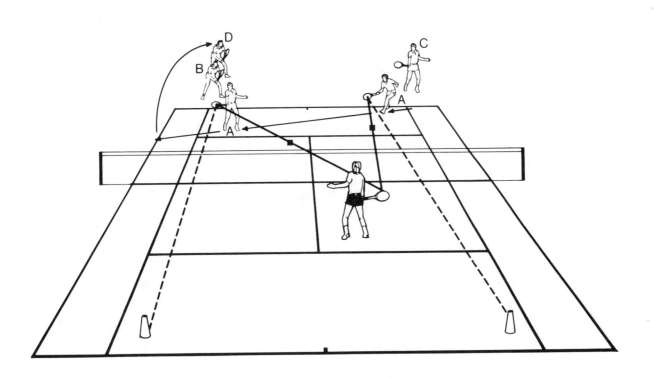

DRILL EIGHT:
Two-ball crisscross.
OBJECTIVE:
To improve groundstrokes and approach shots.

OPERATION

a. Feeder stands at service line.

b. Players *A* and *C* stand in the left corner of the baseline. *B* and *D* stand in the right corner.

c. Feeder hits two balls to *A*'s forehand. *A* hits first ball as a regular groundstroke down the line, the second ball as an approach shot down the line. After this, *A* goes back to the opposite line and waits for his turn to hit backhands.

d. After *A* has hit the two shots, feeder hits two balls to *B*'s backhand. *B* hits the first ball as a groundstroke, and the second as an approach down the lines. This hitter also switches lines.

ALTERNATIVES

1. Alternate hitting first ball crosscourt, second ball down the line.

2. Variation of strokes is also recommended: slice approach shot.

3. Approach and a volley.

4. The drill can easily be varied depending on type of shot wanted, numbers of balls hit, etc.

VOLLEY DRILLS

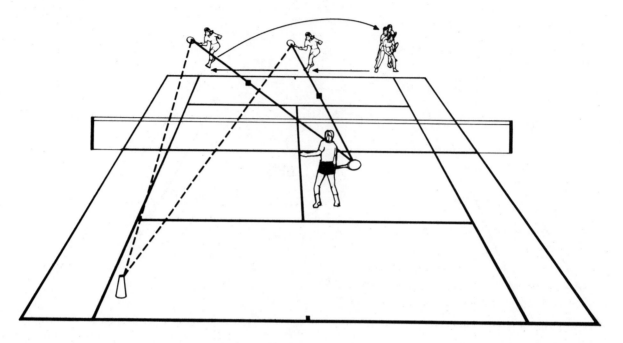

DRILL NINE:
Two balls across.

OPERATION

a. See drill and diagram #1.

b. Players stand at service line on the singles line.

c. Feeder hits the first ball to player's forehand; this first volley should be hit around the service line. After hitting this shot, player should move in about four feet from the net to hit the second forehand volley.

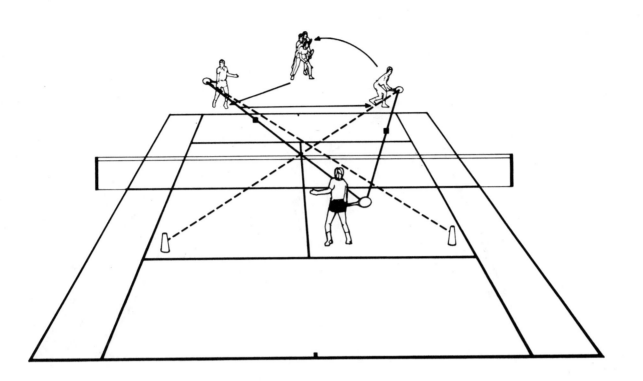

DRILL TEN:
Windshield-wiper volley drill.

OPERATION

a. See drill and diagram #6.
b. Net man *A* stands eight feet from the net on the singles line, while the net man *B* stands eight feet from the net on the center line.

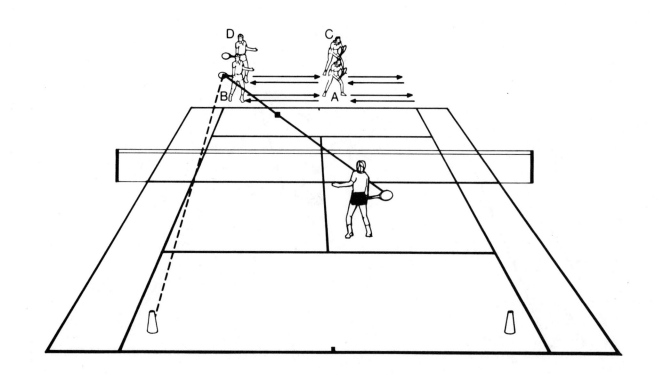

DRILL ELEVEN:
Two-ball crisscross volley.

OPERATION

a. See drill and diagram #7.
b. Players A and C stand in the left corner of
   the service line. B and D stand in the right
   corner.
c. Feeder hits two balls to A's forehand. A hits
   her first volley from the service line, as an
   approach volley down the line, the second
   ball as a put-away crosscourt.
d. The rest of the operation is the same as shown
   in diagram #7.

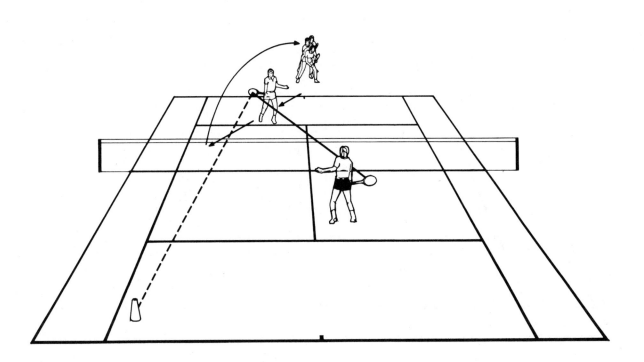

DRILL TWELVE:
High volley.
OBJECTIVE:
To take advantage of the short high balls.

OPERATION

a. Instructor stands at service line.

b. Players stand at center of baseline.

c. Feeder hits a high ball to the first player in line, around the service line. After hitting the high volley, player goes to back of the starting line, and second player starts the drill.

d. It is important to keep players behind the baseline until feeder hits the ball. The players must assume that they are rallying from the baseline, and that the opponent has hit a high moon ball that they are going to attack in the air.

ALTERNATIVES

1. Alternate placement.

2. Alternate strokes.

3. Mix with a groundstroke.

4. Person in front hits a forehand high volley, person behind hits a backhand high volley (this will improve concentration).

5. High volley and a put-away volley.

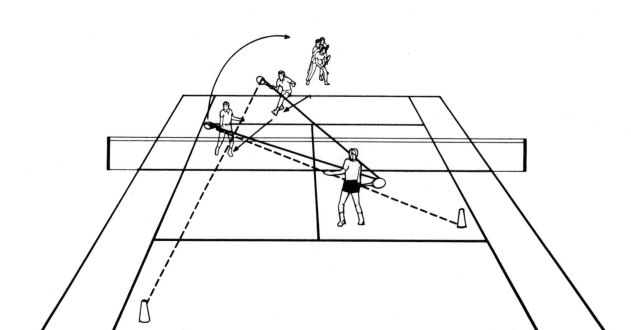

DRILL THIRTEEN
Approach volley and a volley.
OBJECTIVES:
To provide excellent practice for first volleys and
put-away volleys.
To improve footwork.
To get the correct mechanics of following the
approaches to the net.

OPERATION

a. Feeder stands at service line.
b. Players stand at center of baseline.
c. Feeder hits two balls to first player's forehand. Player hits first volley around the
   service line, placing it deep down the line; the
   second ball is hit inside service line as put-
   away angle crosscourt volley. After hitting
   both shots, player goes back to the starting
   line, and second player starts the drill.
d. It is important to make player follow his first
   volley in.
e. Emphasis should be made in placing first
   volley deep.
f. The second ball is a put-away (no touch
   volley).

ALTERNATIVES

1. Use same pattern for backhands.
2. First ball forehand volley, second ball backhand volley, and vice versa.
3. First ball a volley, second ball an overhead.

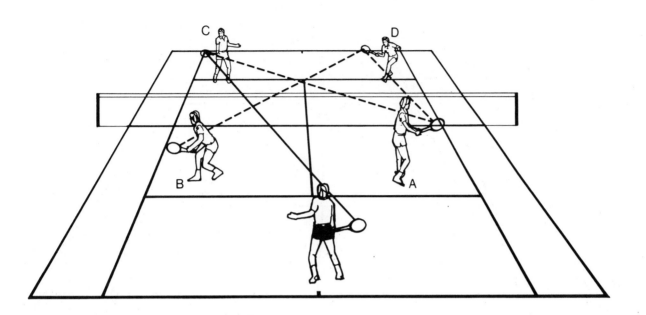

DRILL FOURTEEN:
Two-on-two volley drill.
OBJECTIVES:
To teach students to keep ball in play.
To sharpen reflexes.

OPERATION

a. Instructor stands in the middle of the back court.

b. A and B stand on the service line opposite C and D.

c. Instructor feeds a volley to either C or D. They volley back to either A or B and a rally is begun. Instructor keeps drill moving smoothly while offering instruction.

d. It is important to keep rally going at good pace. No half-volleys should be hit.

e. If there are more than four players, they can rotate in and out.

ALTERNATIVES

1. Move players closer, so they can work on quick angle volleys.

2. Move players back behind service line, so they can work on depth and control.

3. Rally down the lines—A with C and B with D. Then alternate crosscourt—A and D, B and C. All volleys.

DRILL FIFTEEN:
Volleys against the fence.
OBJECTIVES:
To shorten backswing.
To sharpen reflexes.

OPERATION

a. Instructor stands in the middle of the back-court, moving back and forth.
b. Players *A*, *B*, and *C* stand with backs against the back fence.
c. Players *D*, *E*, and *F* stand on the baseline.
d. *A* volleys with *F*, *B* with *E*, and *C* with *D*.
e. After a few minutes of fast, quick volleys, instructor orders a switch, and everybody moves one position to the left. The advantage of switching is that everybody will be against the fence, and with a different partner every time.
f. It is important that players *A*, *B*, and *C* keep backs against the fence.
g. Make players volley with a short and compact motion.

ALTERNATIVE

1. Two-on-one, two-on-baseline, one against the fence.

COMBINATION GROUNDSTROKE AND VOLLEY DRILLS

DRILL SIXTEEN:
Approach shot groundstroke and a volley.
OBJECTIVES:
To make students take advantage of short balls.
To get the correct mechanics of following the approaches to the net.
To place the approach deep and to put the volley away.

OPERATION

a. Feeder stands at service line.

b. Players stand at center of baseline.

c. Feeder hits two balls to first player's forehand. Player hits first ball behind service line as a groundstroke approach down the line. The second ball is hit inside the service line as a put-away crosscourt angle volley.

d. It is important to make the player follow her approach to the net.

e. Emphasis should be on placing the approach deep.

f. The second ball is a put-away volley.

ALTERNATIVES

1. Forehands only.

2. Backhands.

3. Combination forehands and backhands.

4. Make the approach a run-around forehand (forehand weapon development) and then move in for a volley.

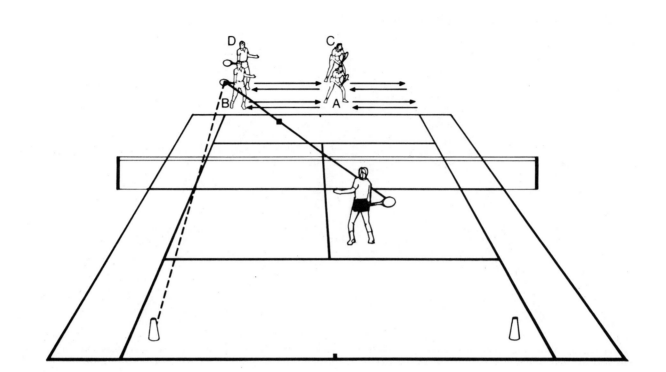

DRILL SEVENTEEN:
Two-ball crisscross approach and a volley.

OPERATION

a. See drill and diagram #7.

b. Feeder hits two balls to A's forehand. A hits his first ball as a groundstroke approach behind the service line, then moves inside the service and hits a forehand volley.

c. The rest of the operation is the same as shown in diagram #7.

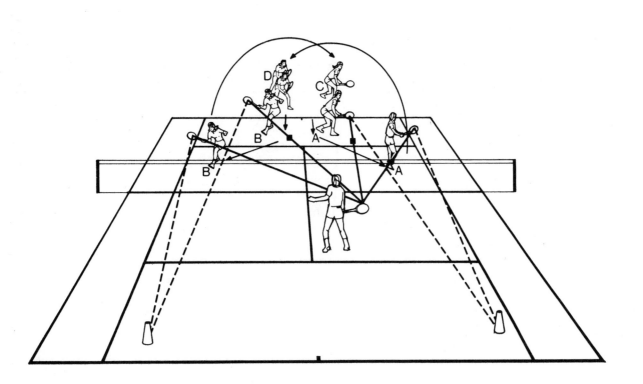

DRILL EIGHTEEN

Two-ball approach drill (two lines).
OBJECTIVES:
To provide excellent practice for approach
groundstrokes and volleys.
To minimize number of courts when there are
many players.

OPERATION

a. Instructor stands at service line.
b. A and C stand just to the left of the center of
   the baseline, and B and D stand just to the
   right.
c. Feeder hits balls to A and B, respectively. A
   hits a backhand approach down the line and
   then closes in for a backhand volley. At the
   same time, B hits a forehand volley. All shots
   must be hit down the line.
d. After hitting, A and B run around the outside
   and switch lines. C and D then step in and the
   exercise is repeated.

ALTERNATIVES

1. Use two instructors on one court.
2. With fewer people, three-ball drill (groundstroke, approach shot, volley).
3. Four balls (groundstroke, approach, volley,
   volley).

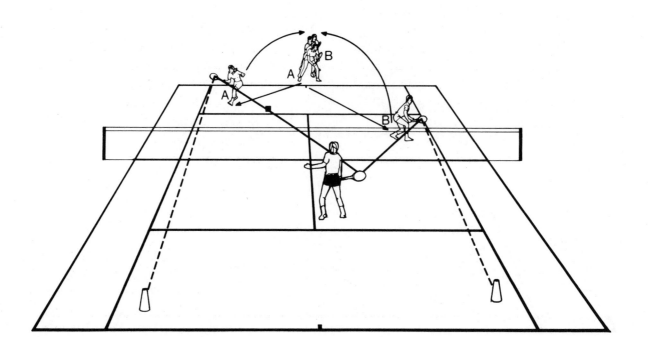

DRILL NINETEEN:
One groundstroke, one volley (one-ball drill).
OBJECTIVES:
To improve concentration.
To improve footwork.

OPERATION

a. Feeder stands at service line.
b. Players stand at center of baseline.
c. Feeder hits the first ball deep to A, who hits a groundstroke down the line. Then feeder hits ball to B who hits a backhand volley down the line.
d. After hitting one shot apiece, A and B run around the outside and go back to the starting line.

ALTERNATIVE

1. All the strokes can be done using this same formation.

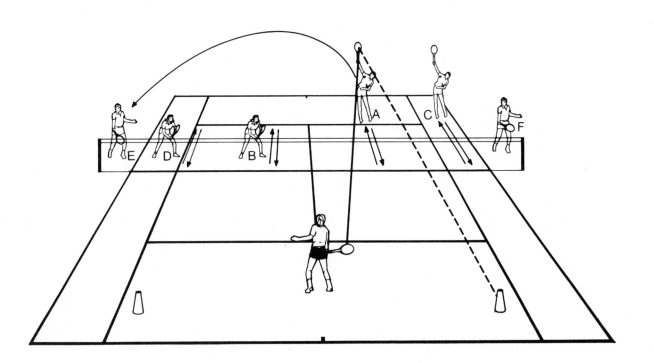

DRILL TWENTY:
Overhead drill.
OBJECTIVES:
To work on the mechanics of the stroke.
To improve consistency and control.

OPERATION

a. Instructor stands just inside the center of the baseline.

b. A stands on the left at the net; B stands in the center of the right service box. C and D stand on the doubles alley parallel to A and B. F and E stand outside of the doubles alley and close to the net.

c. Feeder hits A a lob. As A slides back to hit the overhead, B moves in and touches the net. After A hits the overhead, B slides back to receive a lob fed by instructor; as B hits the overhead, A moves back in to touch the net.

d. Exercise is repeated for two shots.

e. C and D move parallel to A and B, shadowing their movements.

f. F and E jog in place.

g. After two shots, C and D move in and become the hitters, while F and E move inside the doubles alley and become the "shadowers."

h. A and B move out to the opposite side and take places of F and E, jogging in place.

i. It is important for safety that after hitters have executed both shots and are switching lines, they go all the way to the back fence.

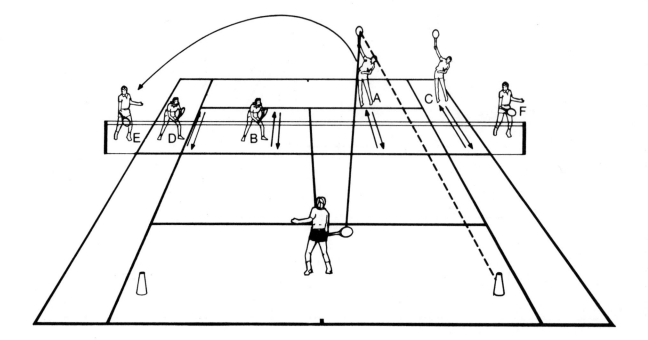

DRILL TWENTY-ONE:
Overhead and attack.

OPERATION

a. Use drill and diagram #20.
b. First ball is a lob, second ball a volley (two balls per person).
c. This drill makes the student move in after hitting the overhead.

DRILL TWENTY-TWO:
One-on-one overhead.

OPERATION

a. Feeder starts at baseline.
b. Player starts close to the net. Player touches the net every time and then slides back to hit the overhead.
c. After hitting several shots, player moves back to the service line. Feeder hits lob near baseline so player has to jump to hit the high deep overhead.
d. Rotate players after several shots.

DRILL FOR SERVES

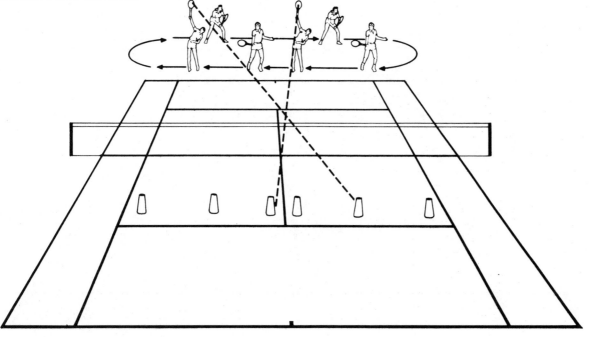

DRILL TWENTY-THREE:

Serve.

OBJECTIVES:

To improve mechanics of the stroke.

To improve consistency and control.

OPERATION

a. Students serving stand behind baseline.

b. Instructor stands behind students.

c. Students waiting stand by the back fence.

d. While the instructor checks the serves, the waiting students toss balls to the servers.

e. After several serves, the instructor commands to rotate, and everybody rotates one position to the right.

f. Continue the procedure through the whole basket.

ALTERNATIVES

1. Let students serve several times with open stance. This will make them rotate the hips.

2. Let students serve from a kneeling position. This will make them hit up on the ball.

ADVANCED DRILLS

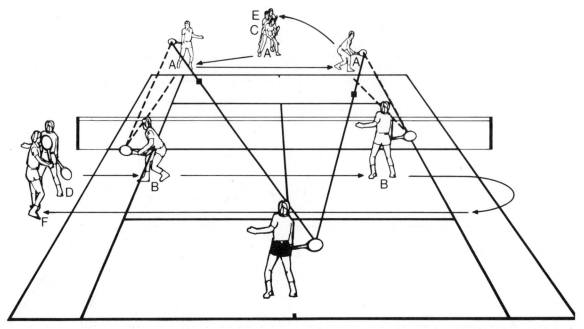

DRILL TWENTY-FOUR:
Follow-the-leader groundstroke volley drill.
OBJECTIVES:
To improve control.
To improve reflexes.
To improve footwork.

OPERATION

a. Instructor stands behind the service line.
b. *A* stands behind the baseline.
c. *B* stands eight feet from the net.
d. Instructor feeds the ball to *A*'s forehand. *A* moves to return the ball down the line to *B*. *B* volleys *A*'s return down the line.
e. Instructor then hits to *A*'s backhand, and *A* moves to return the ball down the line; *B* moves across to cut off the down-the-line shot with a down-the-line forehand volley.
f. Exercise is repeated for two shots.
g. After *A* and *B* hit both shots, they go back to starting line and *C* and *D* go through the drill.

h. After several shots, rotate the players; groundstrokers (*A*, *C*, and *E*) will hit volleys and volleyers (*B*, *D*, and *F*) will hit groundstrokes.

ALTERNATIVE

1. A simple variation of the drill has *A* and *B* hitting crosscourts.

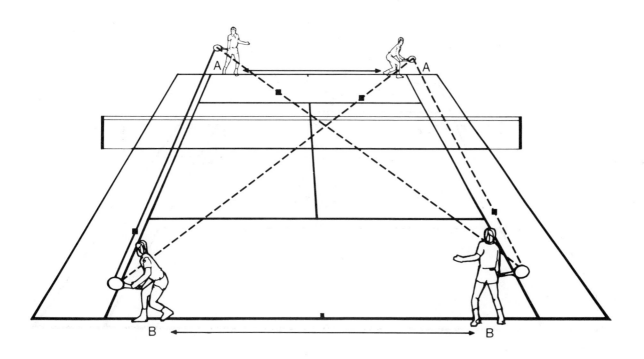

DRILL TWENTY-FIVE:
One-on-one groundstroke drill.
OBJECTIVES:
To improve consistency, control, and footwork.

OPERATION

a. This drill can be done with or without an instructor present.

b. *A* and *B* stand opposite each other behind the baseline.

c. *A* starts by hitting a deep forehand down the line. *B* moves over and hits a deep backhand crosscourt. *A* runs back across and returns *B's* backhand down the line while *B* moves over and returns it with a crosscourt forehand. After several minutes, the drill can be varied so that *A* hits all balls crosscourt, and *B* hits down the line.

d. Stress movement, placement, and depth.

ALTERNATIVE

1. This exercise can be adapted to suit four players. One side hits down the line and the other hits crosscourts. After several minutes, alternate hitting directions.

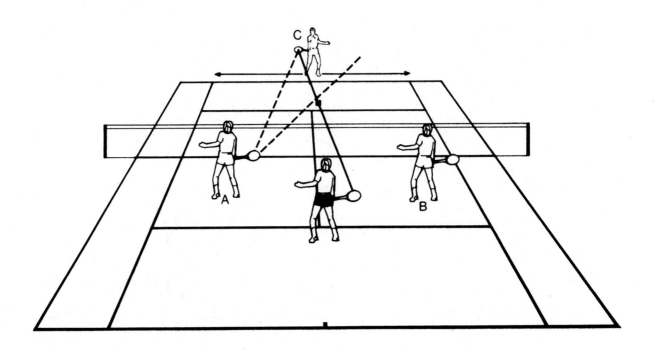

DRILL TWENTY-SIX:
Two-on-one.
OBJECTIVES:
To provide an excellent workout for the student.
To help mobility and anticipation.

OPERATION

a. Instructor stands behind the middle of the service line.
b. A and B are in the service boxes, and C waits beyond the center of the baseline.
c. Instructor feeds a deep ball to C, who hits a groundstroke to either A or B. They volley it back to C and a rally is begun. A and B must place their volleys so that C is forced to move quickly.
d. Instructor makes sure that the drill moves smoothly while offering instruction. After several minutes, C becomes a volleyer, B becomes the baseliner, and A replaces B. Repeat several times.

e. Make sure that baseliner does not overhit the ball. Baseliner should also work on angles, changes of pace, etc.

ALTERNATIVE

1. A two-on-one volley drill is also excellent. Move everybody to the net, and let them exchange quick volleys.

DRILL TWENTY-SEVEN:
Rotating doubles.
OBJECTIVES:
To simulate actual point play and, at the same
time, keep a number of students involved.

OPERATION

a. *A, B,* and *C* are the serving team, and *D, E,*
   and *F* are the receiving team. *A* serves to *D,*
   and the point is played out. After that point,
   A moves up to the volley position. *B* moves
   out, and *C* moves in and serves from the same
   side. The other team also rotates counterclockwise: *D* moves up, *E* moves out, and *F*
   becomes the receiver.

b. In this drill, we stress serving and volleying,
   good returns, closing in on the net, and good
   teamwork, movement, communication, etc.

ALTERNATIVE

1. *Rotating singles:* Using the same teams, *A, B,*
   and *C* will be the servers and *D, E,* and *F* the
   returners. After the point is played, the
   winner stays in and the loser rotates out. It is
   helpful to set a maximum of three times a
   winner can stay in. The students should play a
   game to 21; at 11 they switch sides, and the
   returners become the servers. We usually play
   two of three games to 21.

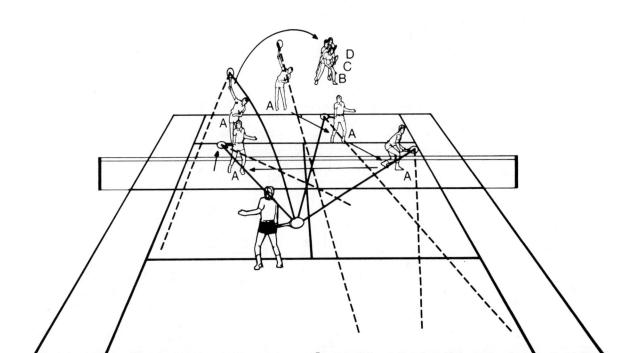

DRILL TWENTY-EIGHT:
Serve-and-volley drill.
OBJECTIVE:
To make players comfortable with the attack
game.

OPERATION

a. Instructor stands on the left, just behind the
   service line.
b. A stands ready to serve on the deuce side.
c. A serves the ball and follows it into the net.
   Instructor feeds three volleys to A. A hits the
   first volley deep to a corner, and then moves
   in for backhand and a forehand put-away
   volley.
d. Instructor then feeds a lob and A puts the
   overhead away.
e. B then moves in and follows the same routine.
   Exercise is repeated for several turns.

ALTERNATIVE

1. This drill can be varied by changing the
   number of balls (with a large group, use two-
   ball drill), the order, etc.

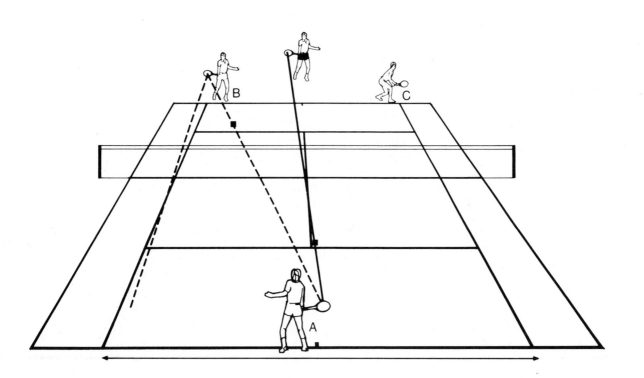

DRILL TWENTY-NINE:
Two-on-one from the baseline.
OBJECTIVE:
To improve consistency and mobility.

OPERATION

a. Instructor stands close to back fence and behind hitters *B* and C.

b. *B* and C stand opposite *A*, behind the baseline.

c. Instructor hits the ball to *A*, and *A* hits crosscourt to *B*'s forehand; *B* hits down the line, and *A* moves over and hits a backhand down the line to *A*'s forehand. After several minutes, they switch clockwise.

d. It is important to keep the ball in play, and to place it deep.

ALTERNATIVE

1. After everybody goes through the drill a few times, *A* hits down the line and *B* and C hit crosscourt.

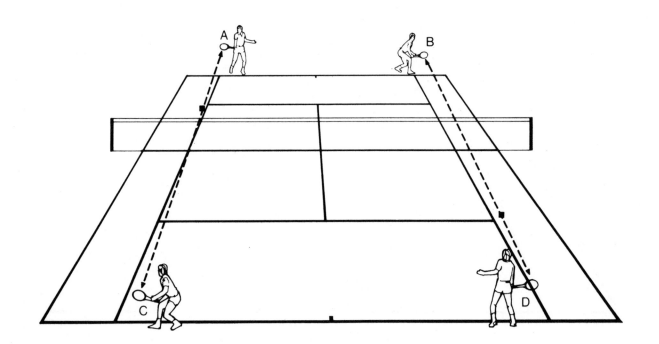

DRILL THIRTY:
Two-on-two from the baseline.
OBJECTIVE:
To develop control and consistency.

OPERATION

a. Players A and B stand opposite C and D, behind the baseline.
b. This drill is excellent for starting practice. For 10 minutes, players hit down the lines (A hits forehands, C hits backhands). After that, they hit crosscourts, forehand to forehand, backhand to backhand.
c. It is important that they keep the ball in play deep. Don't let players overhit.

ALTERNATIVE

1. After several minutes of down-the-lines and crosscourts, move C and D to the net and let them volley down the line and then crosscourt. After this is done, C and D go back to baseline and A and B move into the net.

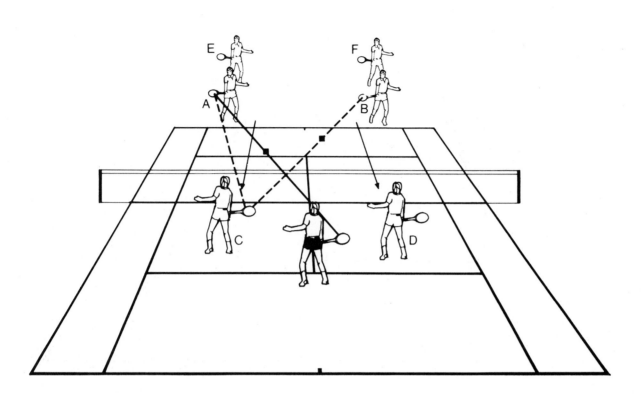

DRILL THIRTY-ONE: Two-on-two approach drill.
OBJECTIVE: Sharpen reflexes and approach shots.

OPERATION

a. Instructor stands behind the center of the service line.
b. One team stands at baseline (A, B), opposing team at the net (C, D).
c. Ball is put into play by instructor.
d. A or B hits the approach shot and both move into net, playing out the point. After the point is played, A and B move back and take E and F's position. E and F play out the point.
e. When one of the baseline teams scores five points, it takes the net, and the volleyers move to the baseline.

ALTERNATIVE

1. Just volleys. Instructor feeds ball and the team takes it as an approach volley.

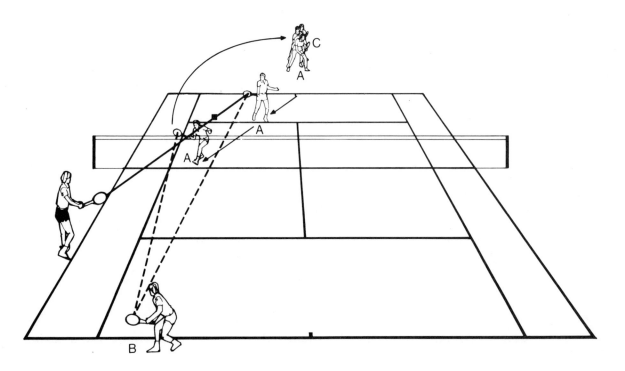

DRILL THIRTY-TWO: King of the court.
OBJECTIVE: To sharpen volleys and passing
shots.

OPERATION

a. Instructor stands outside the doubles alley.
b. *A* waits on baseline, as does opponent *B*.
   Instructor feeds ball to *A*, who hits an approach and moves to the net. *B* tries to pass
   A at the net. After point is over, *A* goes to
   back of starting line and *C* takes *A*'s place.
c. Rotation continues until *A* or *C* wins five
   points from *B*. *A* or *C* then takes *B*'s place.

ALTERNATIVES

1. Make the approach a volley.
2. Make all approaches first with topspin, then
   with slice, etc.

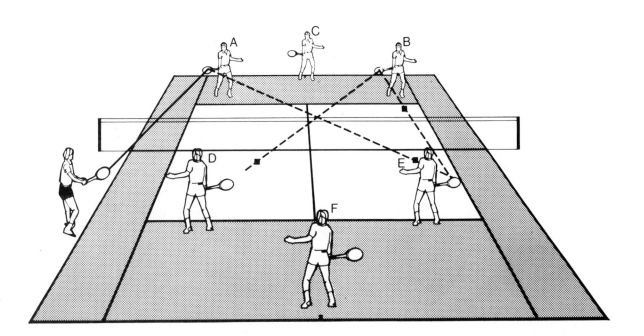

DRILL THIRTY-THREE: Dink game.
OBJECTIVES: To learn to control racquet face.
To work on angles and drop shots.

OPERATION

a. Instructor out of the court, starts every point.
b. A, B, and C are one team, D, E, and F their opponents at the opposite side. A and B start playing against D and E; they only play the service area. As soon as one of the players misses a point, he is out and the player standing by (C or F) replaces him. If a team wins three points consecutively, it must switch. Example: If team A and B wins three points, then B goes out and C moves in. They should play to 21.
c. Make sure players stand on service lines and hit the ball back and forth without overhitting.
d. Make sure they work on racquet control.

ALTERNATIVE

1. An excellent variation to this drill is to place the players in a single line. The person in front hits the first ball and then moves out of the way so the person behind can continue the point.

DRILL THIRTY-FOUR: Height and depth.
OBJECTIVE: To work on groundstroke depth.

OPERATION

a. Instructor outside doubles line, starts every
   point.
b. A, B, and C are one team, D, E, and F their
   opponents at the opposite side. A and B start
   against D and E, C and F wait in the back
   until a teammate makes an error.
c. Instructor feeds the ball to A or B, who must
   hit groundstrokes that land between the
   service line and the baseline (shaded area). If
   the ball does not land in the shaded area, the
   point is lost.
d. Switch sides after a team acquires 11 points.

ALTERNATIVES

1. Same drill, but play singles one player at a
   time!
2. Rather than just losing the point when the ball
   does not land in the shaded area, the players
   attack that short ball, moving to the net.

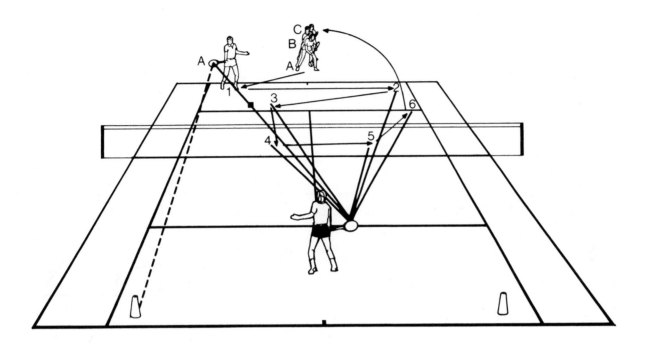

DRILL THIRTY-FIVE: Six-ball drill.
OBJECTIVES: To improve mobility.
To improve mechanics of play situations.

OPERATION

a. Instructor on baseline.
b. Player A behind the center of the baseline.
c. Instructor feeds six balls: two groundstrokes, one approach shot, two volleys, and one overhead. After player A hits the overhead, she goes back to the end of the line and player B starts the drill.

ALTERNATIVES

1. Don't let player know where you are feeding.
2. *Twelve-ball drill:* Same as the six-ball drill, except that the player should let the sixth ball go over her head. The drill then starts all over again, finishing with the twelfth ball, an overhead.

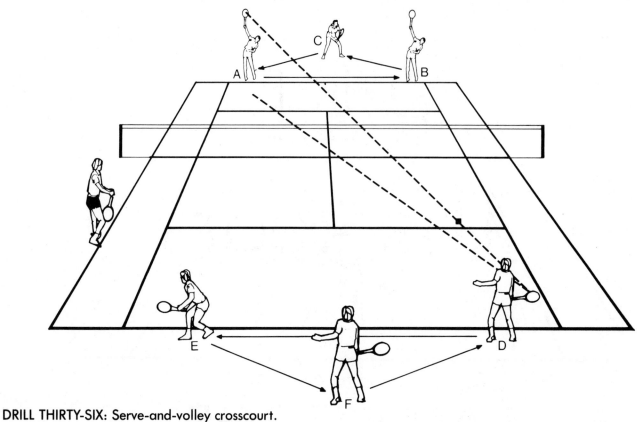

DRILL THIRTY-SIX: Serve-and-volley crosscourt.
OBJECTIVE: To improve the mobility and
mechanics of the serve and volley.
To work on crosscourt returns.
To provide an excellent drill for doubles.

OPERATION

a. Instructor stands outside of sideline.
b. Two groups of players: A, B, C are servers,
   D, E, F receivers.
c. A serves the first ball to D, D returns crosscourt and the point is played crosscourt.
   When the point is over, B serves to E, and
   they also play the point out.

d. After A and B have played the point out, C
   serves and A takes B's place.
e. The returners also rotate: F moves to take D's
   place, and D takes E's place.
f. After several minutes, they switch—the
   returners serve, and vice versa.

THREE

The Years to Greatness

8

STARTING OFF (Eight to Ten)

Throughout my travels and years of teaching in city parks, country clubs, resorts, and now the Academy, the question I have been asked most often by parents is, "When should my kid start?" Hey, that's like asking what is the best age to get married. I say you'll know when the time is right. You'll know when the interest is there. And for better or for worse, through the good times and the bad, your children will be involving themselves in a sport that will demand all of the attention and effort and thought that a marriage requires.

The kids in tennis keep getting younger and younger. That isn't bad by any means. With a big qualification: the interest *must* be there. Let's not make this a shotgun marriage. Don't force the issue. Tennis should be fun from the start! Make certain that children play because *they want to*, not because you expect them to. I've said this earlier and you're probably sick of hearing it. That's the tennis teacher in me. I keep coming back to the fundamentals. So I'll say it again. **MAKE TENNIS FUN.** That's my no. 1 tennis lesson to parents.

One of my students at the Academy is Robin Cifaldi, a youngster who grew up in Hilton Head, S.C. She has told me that she learned the game in a unique way. Sea Pines Plantation had a starter program for the kids called Tiny Tots Tennis. Charlie Ellis, who ran the program, had plywood cutouts of various animals, such as raccoons and alligators and foxes. Charlie fed balls to the little kids, some as young as four years, and they tried to hit them through openings in the animal cutouts. It was great fun! The kids had little informal competitions among themselves. It was play. Even picking up the balls became a game! They tried to see how many balls they could pile onto their racquets.

Even though superstars such as Jimmy Connors, Chris Evert, and Tracy Austin were hitting balls by the age of four, I suggest that a child should begin playing between the ages of six and eight, to allow for some degree of concentration, coordination, and strength.

In all my thousands of young students over the years, early coordination and feeling for the ball has told me a great deal about a child's raw talent. Often I am struck by how athletes' early recollections consistently feature a fascination with balls and playing games with them. They remember how their parents simply rolled a ball to them. The next step would be catching it on a bounce. Then they learned to use a tennis racquet, or a baseball bat, to make contact with the ball. Their parents made it fun.

There's another question I'm asked all the time: "Are champions born or are they made?" I would say that champions are born with certain physical gifts, much like a genius is born with certain mental gifts. Champions have things like exceptional timing—the trademark of an Aaron Krickstein—or the fierce desire to win of a Jimmy Arias. However, a combination of good coaching, hard work, and a total commitment of time and effort also can produce a champion.

Perhaps you have heard a phrase that often comes up in tennis when someone tries to explain why a junior champion never progressed in either college or the pros: "They were too good too soon." The point is that too much emphasis was

Especially with his youngest, Nick stresses fundamentals.

placed on winning and losing at a young age. I prefer to build a strong foundation. Don't worry about rankings at first. Decide what type of game your child will play 10 years in the future and try to develop that game. Give a child the tools and let him or her go to work, but don't build sand castles. Try to build something substantial.

The key to developing a champion, as I've said in the early chapters, is creating a flexible master plan and sticking to it, within reason. "Flexible" is important. Fight the urge to get caught up in the problem of the moment. Too often, parents find that their child has difficulty mastering a certain grip or style of play, so they skip it and try something else. Soon they find themselves patching up their child's game, applying Band-Aids instead of treating the overall problem with work. One day their child is hitting a two-handed backhand, the next day a one-hander. One day he plays with topspin, the next day he's hitting the ball flat. One day Guillermo Vilas, the next Jimmy Connors. Find something that is comfortable, stick with it, build on it.

Though I've never met him, I'm a great admirer of Ben Hogan, the golf champion. This man is one of the most admired fellows in the history of the game. Even today, pro golfers refer to him as "Mr. Hogan." Hogan as a young player was not very good. He won the majority of his titles after years and years of mediocrity. What he did was practice, practice, practice. Years later, long after Hogan had retired, John Mahaffey, a young fellow on the circuit, telephoned "Mr. Hogan." Mahaffey was something of a Hogan protégé: a fellow Texan and a hard worker. On the telephone, Mahaffey complained about his lack of success on the tour. Hogan listened impassively. Finally he spoke.

"You been practicing?"

"Oh yes, Mr. Hogan. I've been practicing every day."

"Practice some more," Hogan said, and hung up.

Vince Lombardi is famous for having said, "Winning isn't everything, it's the only thing." This is one of the few points where Lombardi and I part company. In tennis, giving 110 percent is the only thing. Winning is a tremendous thrill, but in tennis accepting a loss and learning from it is something we all must face. There are no undefeated heavyweight champions in tennis. In every tournament, there are many more losers than winners.

From the start, parents must teach their children how to handle competition. One of my former students is Lori Kosten, who at a young age was virtually unbeatable on a tennis court. Then things changed. Lori's subsequent problems were chronicled in a *Sports Illustrated* article. She talked about how she never could accept losing. Eventually it caused her to give up the game.

I remember Lori telling me how the kids at her school back home in Memphis, Tenn., never understood what she was doing. She would come back from a tournament in which she felt she had done very well. Maybe she had defeated the top seed and reached the semifinals before losing. She had played well. But when she told her classmates, all they could see was that she had lost in the semifinals. Finally, the joy of winning was overcome by the pain of defeat.

If a parent places more emphasis on the outcome of a match than on whether the child gave 100 percent or improved from a previous showing, serious problems may develop. Tournaments are the beginning tennis player's equivalent of taking a school exam. In school, the good student looks forward to an exam, the poor student is filled with trepidation. Likewise, the accomplished tennis player relishes tournament play. The poor players who have not done their homework are filled with dread. Parents must keep a positive approach to their child's inevitable losses. Don't be overly critical. If you do not make a child afraid of losing, the child ultimately will develop a winning game. Competition is the best thing in the world. It compels you to set goals and to work toward them, and it teaches you how to handle pressure and to be self-reliant, lessons that will serve you well forever.

A child is sensitive to failure. We all recall the stereotypical sports outcast, the kid off by himself while the other children are playing games, the boy always chosen last and stuck in right field in sandlot baseball games. When I am confronted with a beginning child who is not enjoying success in a group, I call a halt to practice and take the student aside. I have him take his racquet back and I slowly pitch him balls underhanded. After three or four tries, he begins to make contact, and that is all it takes to get him interested again. A little encouragement and a pat on the back produces a big smile. That's how we turn lemons into lemonade.

I use the same philosophy when teaching the serve to small youngsters. Rather than insisting they begin on the baseline and struggle to get a ball over the net, I bring them up to the service line, tell them to keep their motion smooth and continuous, and allow them to hit the ball over the net from there.

I build on confidence and success. Over the years I have played a game countless times with Carling Bassett. Carling always worked hard, and so I tried to introduce ways to make our workouts more fun yet still productive. I would say to Carling, "I'll bet you can't hit thirty balls over without a miss." This would get her competitive instinct going. She was always determined to prove me wrong. I would keep increasing the quota, and each time as she would reach it, she would smile and say, "Beat you again, Nick."

It may seem funny now, but I used to be a card-carrying member of the Old School, as stodgy and stilted in my thinking as anyone. My way was the right way, the only way. I had to learn—and my teacher turned out to be, as implausible as it sounds, a Cuban immigrant who had learned tennis out of a book. Tony Arias taught his son, Jimmy, to play, and taught him in Buffalo, N.Y., hardly the tennis capital of the world. From the beginning, Tony insisted on a long, smooth, relaxed stroke from his son. His philosophy was to "hit the ball" and not worry so much about accuracy. This simple idea shaped Jimmy's success later.

When I began teaching in the late fifties, I did so according to the Establishment. For decades, tennis had been taught in the classical style, emphasizing long elegant strokes. I can remember the shock when we heard that a gentleman in Ft. Lauderdale actually was so foolish as to teach his daughter a two-handed backhand—Jimmy Evert and his daughter, Chris.

Before then, before Tony and Jimmy Arias came into my life, I was the city pro for the North Miami Beach Recreation Department. One young boy about 10 years old caught my eye. He never said a word, ran down every ball, and was always the first to arrive and the last to leave. Hmmmm. Might be some raw material here, I thought.

His name was Brian Gottfried, and we became a team. Since I was still relatively new to tennis, I paid little attention to his grip. Brian hit his forehand while holding the racquet as if he were shaking hands with it. On his backhand, he moved a little to the left. He had no real problem, however, so I left him alone.

From the beginning, Brian spent as much time as possible volleying. The grip he used was much the same as the one he

Brian Gottfried's Continental forehand.

used for his forehand and for his serves and the overhead—the Continental—and it was the grip I pushed with Brian as he progressed up the ladder, reaching a position of no. 4 in the world.

Although I still believe that the Continental grip is a good grip for volleying, I feel that it is very limiting on the forehand. If I had known then what I know now, I would have changed Brian Gottfried's grip to something that would have allowed him to develop a weapon more in the style of Jimmy Arias. Jimmy has a Semi-Western forehand (see p. 149); his hand is turned to the right so that as he hits the ball, he brushes up its back, imparting topspin. It's difficult to do this with the Continental. As a youngster gets older and the pace and power of his competitors' games increase, he needs to be able to match force with force. It became a problem for Brian Gottfried, one he overcame with exceptional volleying and great athleticism. By the same token, Jimmy Arias can blow you off the court with his forehand. I may be putting myself out on a limb, but I believe that Brian's determination, if combined with a forehand weapon similar to Jimmy's, would have resulted in several world championships for Brian.

Jimmy's stroke, taught to him by his father, convinced me that the old "straight arm, no wrist acceleration, racquet head above the wrist, point in the direction you are hitting" days are over. *There is no one correct style of play.* These days, in working with youngsters just learning the game, I say very little about grips, footwork, and the like. My goals are more general:

1. Motivate.
2. Get students to enjoy the lessons.
3. Establish very few initial goals other than to try one's best.
4. Work on a few simple basics, but let them develop their own style.
5. Talk to them about sportsmanship.
6. Make sure they leave the court happy and excited.

Keeping these ideas in mind, I proceed with simple games of pitching balls and playing catch, at first without the racquet. I don't worry about stroke production, grips, and so on. I don't want to fill my new students' minds with too much information. A simple approach with total beginners goes as follows:

Jimmy Arias's
Semi-Western forehand.

NICK:
You all did a great job playing our pitch-catch games, but now [in a joking manner] I'm going to get you. I'll bet you can't do what I do. I'm standing with my racquet out front and I am going to watch the ball at all times. See how I watch the ball, following it as it hits my strings.

This is a very simple yet effective method of introducing beginners to the ready position, and to the importance of watching the ball. After a little of this, I have the children imitate me. I toss each ball softly to them. No way do I yet go into any specifics about backswings, follow-throughs, etc. My objective is to have each student contact the ball. Where it goes is secondary. I make sure I praise everyone. I gauge their eye-hand coordination, and make mental notes on whether it needs work. Above all, I am not concerned with having the students hit in any particular way.

After they have developed a certain proficiency and are able to make regular contact with the ball, I give them fundamentals. I show them the ready position, the forehand grip, a one-hand backhand and a two-hand backhand, the motion for the serve and the overhead; I demonstrate the volley and the drop shot.

This sudden, all-at-once approach is important, because I want the students to see tennis as a total game from the start, not simply a forehand and a backhand from the baseline. I want them to develop outstanding groundstrokes, to be sure—techniques similar to those of Jimmy Arias or Carling Bassett—but at the same time I want them to have a sense of net play and of the serve.

Tony Arias and Dr. Herb Krickstein have done remarkable jobs on, respectively, Jimmy Arias's forehand and the groundstrokes of Aaron Krickstein. Even so, I still have to practically pull both of them to the net. Both have improved their volleys, which will get better still, but these deficiencies might have been avoided if their early work had emphasized the importance of ending the point at the net.

After a youngster begins working on the rudiments of the game, within a short period she will start to develop her own style of play. This is the time when the coach should place more emphasis on the grip, backswing, and follow-through, and on weight balance and the height by which the ball clears the net.

Your first big decision when coaching beginners will concern the two-handed backhand. Do you want it or not? I would say this: A two-hander learned from the beginning can be adapted later, especially if it is taught with a one-hand release—that is, if the player releases the racquet after making contact with the ball (see pp. 90-91).

This is only the first of countless decisions that must be made about a child's tennis game. Either of two general approaches should be followed. Decide which you want to build:

1. Conservative strokes—the type that promote consistency, thereby allowing you to outsteady an opponent. (This is the game favored by baseliners.)
2. Power strokes—free-swinging, with a lot of sting on the ball. These produce less consistency, more errors—and without doubt, more defeats in the early going.

I once read a book by Arnold Palmer in which he advocated teaching children how to play golf by having them swing hard on every drive. His theory was that you could later learn to swing easy, but that it is more difficult to learn how to hit the ball far.

In tennis, you more or less have to stick with one style if you are to succeed. Generally, I favor the Power Game over one

Developing eye-hand coordination, casually.

that strives for absolute consistency. I want to see a player attack at the first opportunity. The majority of our daily drills emphasize going for winners, and clearing the net. Rarely do my students hear me yell about a shot that goes over the baseline, but let a ball plunk into the net and I go crazy. "How can your opponent make a mistake when you hit the ball into the net?" I yell. "Hit it over the net. So it's long—at least you'll give him a chance to swing at it and make an error."

In the Power Game, it is important to develop a big weapon from the beginning. If you look at the top players coming up today, you'll see that each has a big weapon. Ivan Lendl crunches his forehand; John McEnroe's serve is awesome. But at the same time, I must again emphasize the development of the weaker parts of a game. Ask a kid what his favorite shot is and he will tell you the stroke at which he's most competent. It's like reading an astrology column. You get only the positive characteristics, not the negative ones. Ask a kid what his least favorite shot is, and you'll discover the one that needs practice.

As the child develops, certain stroking patterns will emerge. The important thing is to strive for smoothness through the ball. You also have to consider whether you want a looped forehand—one in which the racquet head is taken back high, then dropped down and brought up and through the ball—or a straight-back forehand in which the racquet is taken straight back, gets underneath the ball, and then comes straight out through the ball (see pp. 80-83). I tend to lean toward the looped backswing, because it involves a continuous motion and thus produces more power.

Although players such as Stan Smith and Brian Gottfried— the classical stylists—have good luck with a shortened follow-through, the trend among newer players is to be longer and looser with this segment of the stroke. Letting the racquet go right on through and around after contact actually aids in developing a weapon. Jimmy Arias, Ivan Lendl, and Bjorn Borg are three proponents of the Power Game who use this kind of looseness in forehand strokes.

Let's now review some of the strokes of special concern to the young beginner.

If a child does begin with a **one-hand backhand,** be sure the nonhitting hand is used to help make the grip change, moving the hand over to the backhand side, and also that the nonhitting hand is used to guide the racquet back. The arm can be fairly close to the body on the backswing. In the forward part of the swing, the student should get the racquet head below the ball and hit up through it and out. The idea is to be firm, yet relaxed.

With the **two-handed backhand,** there are two basic grips. The first places both hands together in Eastern forehand style. This provides equal strength from both hands and allows the student to guide the ball with the stroke. This backhand gets the arms and elbows away from the body and extends them out *in front* on the follow-through in the direction you want the ball to go. Tracy Austin and Chris Evert are masters of this stroke. The other grip has the bottom hand in a Continental grip while the other hand remains in an Eastern forehand. With this grip, you have more versatility since you are able to let go on wide balls, drop shots, low slices, and volleys.

The above backhands have several options on the follow-through. These include:

1. Arms extended out toward the target.
2. Arms extended out toward the target with the elbows bending at full extension and then around the shoulder with firm wrists.
3. Finally, the tremendous wrist acceleration on contact such as that utilized by Borg and Andrea Temasvari, which results in excessive topspin.

Good beginnings.

Grip for the
two-handed backhand.

Another type of basic **backhand** was referred to in Chapter 6 as the backhand of the future: the two-hander with a one-hand follow-through. Just after contact, the player releases the top hand, allowing for an easier follow-through. This is the stroke that Andrea Jaeger employs so well. It gives a player more reach, is more effective for topspin, works quite well on your volleys and drop shots, and is better adapted to slice and chip shots.

On the **serve,** many beginners are not strong enough to use the proper backhand grip. They will find it easier to use a forehand grip in the beginning, and then, after they have mastered the serving motion, to switch to the backhand grip, thereby allowing for more spin on the serve. At the outset, the greatest emphasis should be placed on developing rhythm and timing with the ball and racquet. From smoothness comes power. One tip that seems to help in developing a serve is to begin the motion with the racquet already behind the head, elbow-high. This allows students to feel the position they are trying to achieve just before beginning the forward part of the swing, throwing the racquet up and out.

As the serve develops, make certain that the student's toss continues to be out in front. Work on the wrist snap and racquet acceleration for power. Also emphasize the long, smooth follow-through.

The **volley** is the simplest stroke in tennis, yet it is one of the more difficult to master. Let the student develop his volley with his own grip in the beginning, emphasizing the shoulder turn that allows him to meet the ball out in front with a short, firm swing—a "punching motion," as most people call it. As players gain strength, they should begin to realize the need for one grip on the volley, using the Continental on both forehand and backhand. Most likely, the two-hand backhand players also will discover that their volleys will be more versatile if they can make them with only one hand. However, there have been many successful two-handed volleyers (i.e., Jimmy Connors, Frew McMillan).

The final fundamentals are the overhead and the drop shot, sort of the salad dressing of one's game. They could not be less alike—one is powerful, the other deceptive—yet both can consistently be outright winners if played correctly.

I find it helpful to place my young students at the net when they are learning the overhead. Eliminate the backswing. Have them get the racquet behind the head, with elbows up. Keep the head up, watch the ball by tracking it with an extended left hand, and snap out through with full extension and a good follow-through. Be sure to eliminate excess body motions.

There is a simple drill I have found invaluable in teaching the drop shot to youngsters. I call it "mini-tennis," a game that is played totally within the service boxes. In order for the students to keep the ball in play, they have to develop both concentration and good touch. "Mini-tennis" is a fun way of working on control, rather than power.

Anytime you work with a beginner on fundamentals, you are going to experience a certain amount of frustration at your student's mistakes. I maintain that you should concentrate on one thing at a time. Keep comments short and stick to one problem. When you have conquered that fault, move on to another. Don't give the student more than he or she can think about.

No doubt the biggest problem you'll face will be how to handle failure. I recommend strongly that coach, parent, and student keep open lines of communication. Consider the commitment to tennis seriously. Evaluate the commitment at least every year, and plan for the future. Remember, you can go only so far as you are willing to go, and the journey will be immeasurably easier if you keep in mind that ultimately tennis is a game played for love, not money.

Another day well done.

9

THE LEARNING PHASE
(Ten to Twelve)

As player and parent progress through the early years of junior tennis, they will discover that there's something new around almost every corner. For instance, how do you deal with envy or jealousy? In junior tennis, these emotions are as prevalent as the sun at dawn. The ranking system of the sport is so total, so absolute, that it's almost natural for children to find some form of rancor from below when they are near the top, or feel it themselves if they are near the bottom. My friend Louis Marx tells me that the same thing occurs in his oil business. "I think I'm well liked by my competitors," Louis has said to me. "But by the same token, I realize that they probably are a little happy when one of my wells comes up empty. 'Better him than me,' they think."

Here is a chance for children to gain some insight into human nature that will stay with them forever. Misery loves company. Young tennis players shouldn't be surprised to notice that some of their friends seem to take a small amount of pleasure from their failures. This is a game in which hard work breeds success. It's part of a parent's job to show their kids that people who do not work as hard find it easy to envy those who do.

Players in the years from 10 to 12, along with working on groundstrokes, must also consider several other facets of on-court behavior. What about cheating, or sportsmanship?

Cheating is a fact of life in junior tennis. Players call their own lines, for the most part, and the inclination is to fudge a bit on the close ones. My advice to my own students is this: Don't do it. And if it happens to you, don't let it affect your play negatively. If you cheat, ultimately you are only cheating yourself. A few years ago I was at a professional tournament, watching a practice match between two players. One was a young star, a player most people agreed was headed for the top. The other was a fellow a couple of years older, someone who had reached a level just above mediocrity in the pro ranks, a guy who was not going to go much further. The younger pro was playing on the side closest to me. I was right behind him, not more than five feet away. His opponent hit a fabulous shot, and the young pro moved to get it, but it was by him in a flash. "Out," he called. Clearly the ball was in. The court was a clay surface, newly maintained, and the ball had left a visible slash well inside the baseline. I could see it from where I stood. The young pro couldn't have missed it. So here was a fellow who cheated even in practice! To me that showed a lack of character, an inability to accept the reality of a situation. Not surprisingly, that fellow never made it to the top. He had the talent, but he was unwilling to make the commitment. I predict that within two years he will be out of tennis.

So as I continually tell my younger players, you are better off calling the close balls good. You are building toward the future. Don't worry about line calls.

What do you do when it is obvious that your opponent is cheating you in a tournament? The first and paramount rule is not to let it affect your play. Keep your concentration. If the cheating continues, there is one simple alternative. Walk to the net and motion your opponent to join you. You then tell the cheater, "You know as well as I that last ball was good. You called it out. You've been hooking me the entire match. If you do it again, on the very next ball you hit, no matter where it lands, I'm calling it out. Now are we going to play tennis or aren't we?"

Sportsmanship is a quality to develop when young. Not only will it make your child a more agreeable person to be around, but it also will help his or her tennis in the future. The trend now, as I see it, is to eliminate the boorish behavior that so many of the stars have gotten away with in the last five years or so. There is a concerted effort to eliminate the outbursts, the abuse of linespeople, the racquet throwing, and all of the petulant and childish behavior that has too often obscured some excellent tennis over recent years. Pro tennis officials have instituted a series of penalties both on and off the court, corresponding to an official Code of Conduct (see p. 163) that gives great latitude to tournament referees to fine or even default players who fail to adhere to its standards. I see this trend continuing, with the penalties becoming even more severe. The players who get into the habit of callous behavior during junior tournaments are all too apt later, in college or pro events, to find themselves losing matches because of it. And parents—don't think that stifling your child's emotions will in any way affect his or her tennis negatively. In fact, much the opposite will occur. Toning down the outbursts can only help a player's concentration. As proof, I offer Bjorn Borg, the man who won Wimbledon five consecutive times. Borg rarely displayed any emotion beyond a small smile when he played. He learned this attitude as a young boy in Sweden—learned it painfully, when because of a hot temper his tennis federation suspended him from tournament play. Borg learned to be cool while learning to be great.

We spoke a bit about competition in the last chapter. Competition can be the nectar that keeps your interest as you progress in junior tennis, especially around this age, when you get into city and regional tournaments we'll describe in the next part. Lisa Bonder, now knocking on the door to greatness in the women's ranks, found that tournament matches were the most fun for her when she began playing the game. "We had a good junior program," Lisa says, "and occasionally we would get together as a group and go down to Chicago and play team matches. We had a great time."

It is very important that kids approach tournaments with a positive attitude. Excitement and fear are similar emotions. I tell my younger students not to confuse one with the other. Excitement is a positive emotion, one that will help you to new levels of play. Fear can be crippling. Children should learn to channel their excitement through concentration, playing each point one stroke at a time.

Parents also will need to monitor their own behavior at tournaments. Naturally, you will want to watch your child in competition, but try at all costs to be as unobtrusive as possible. Wild displays of partisanship can be as embarrassing to your child as they will ultimately be to you. There is no question that your child will be acutely aware of your presence and how you conduct yourself, no matter how low-key you try to be. In a book I wrote with Julie Anthony, *A Winning Combination,* Julie recalls how her mother once attended one of her matches. As usual, Mrs. Anthony was wearing silk stockings. "Every time I missed or came close to missing a shot, my mother would cross or uncross her legs," Julie says in our book. "Unnoticed by her, but louder than a bomb to me, was the sound of her stockings rubbing against each other when she would cross her legs. So even before a rally was over, I'd know by the sound of her stockings which shots she thought I wouldn't get. Without realizing it at all, my mother had created quite a distraction for me. I won that day, but I asked her not to wear stockings to any more of my matches."

Julie Anthony, with the support of her mother, went on to become a world-class professional. She also became a clinical psychologist, partly because she was fascinated with parent-child relationships in junior tennis. My advice for parents at tournaments is to stay as far in the background as you can be—and then to move back a little farther. Above all—don't wear silk stockings!

Tournaments are the checkups we at the Academy use to gauge a player's progress, but the meat of our program for preadolescents is the day-to-day drilling. A preadolescent player shouldn't worry so much about playing practice matches. The important thing at that age is to develop good groundstrokes, to maintain good habits, and to work on any flaws. If you're coaching kids, try to make them winners in their workouts. Too often players finish on the wrong note, hitting a clinker rather than a winner. For instance, how often have you watched someone hit overheads before a match? Usually, they hit a few and when they miss they say, "That's enough." They hit until they miss, and then quit. Instead, they should try to put away the last ball. Watch pro basketball players. See how many of them are careful always to make their final shots in pregame workouts.

Groove those groundstrokes. Strive for consistency, hitting the ball deep and with pace. One of our favorite drills at the Academy is the two-on-one drill (see p. 130), which teaches mobility and how to play under pressure. One player is on the baseline, and two players are at the net. The baseliner runs down every ball and tries to hit passing shots. The players at the net volley. You must keep the ball moving. If someone misses, another ball must be put into play immediately. Make the baseliner move continuously. This builds up stamina and also teaches players to cope with hitting shots on the run.

A variation on this drill is the two-on-one with all the players on the baseline. Now the lone player hits every shot down the line, while the team on the other side hits every shot crosscourt. This forces the single player to run quite a bit, and it teaches all of the players the importance of learning how to "open up the court," which involves nothing more than hitting a shot that leaves your opponent out of position for the next shot. Once again, it is important to keep the ball moving. If someone misses, another ball must be put in play immediately.

Another drill that is quite effective for a child's early development is the 100-ball drill. Here the idea is to rally, hitting 100 consecutive shots on which the ball lands between the service line and the baseline. Miss once and you have to start over. This teaches depth and the importance of clearing the net by a safe margin.

Some of the Academy's youngest students practice their volleys.

As kids work on the baseline game, however, they should not neglect the game at the net. Get to the net and punch away those volleys!

To review the volley, remember the key points: Get into a good ready position when at the net, almost like a hockey goaltender anticipating the puck. Have your feet spread apart at shoulder width. Relax your knees, to enable you to step into the shot. And keep your racquet out in front, with elbows away from the body, so that with a good shoulder turn you will only have to make a quick punching motion to put away the ball. To emphasize these points, I want you to listen in on one of my lessons at the Academy.

NICK:
Billy, come up to the net, I want to speak to you. [I hit him a volley.]

BILLY:
Why are you hitting balls right at me when you said to come up to talk to you?

NICK:
To show you the proper way of hitting a volley. [Volley.] There, you just did it.

BILLY:
All I did was block the ball.

NICK:
That's great. Why didn't you swing at it as you do with your ground-strokes?

BILLY:
I didn't have time. The ball was at me before I knew it and the only way to block it was by holding my racquet up.

NICK:
You just hit your first volley—blocking the ball. To be a good volleyer you must be alert at all times. Watch the ball leave the opponent's racquet to determine whether it is a forehand or backhand and immediately prepare to block it from that side with a firm wrist.

BILLY:
What grip should I use?

NICK:
For our first few lessons, use the very same grip you use on your forehands and backhands.

BILLY:

I like that. Some of the kids said they had to learn one grip for their volleys, the one you said is called the Continental.

NICK:

What did they think about that?

BILLY:

They had different opinions. Some of the younger kids liked changing their grip because they felt very weak with the Continental grip. Others felt the grip change took too much time.

NICK:

Well, both sides are correct. Later, you can change to the Continental grip, too. But right now, I think you'll get a better feel for the volley if you switch your grips. You're hitting your forehand volley very well, now let's try the backhand. [Volley.]

BILLY:

That's not fair. You said it was coming to my backhand so I changed my grip and you hit it to my forehand. I didn't have time to change back.

NICK:

You'll find that very same thing happening in matches. You must be very alert to switch your grip.

BILLY:

Let's try it.

NICK:

I'll feed one ball at a time going back and forth to forehand and backhand. Ready? [Volley.] That's good. Try turning your shoulder a little more. Use your left hand to hold the throat of the racquet, especially when on the backhand side. It will give you more strength.

BILLY:

That feels good, but I just don't think I have much strength on my backhand volley.

NICK:

In time you'll get stronger. Meeting the ball in front will make up for the loss of strength.

BILLY:

Why do so many of my balls go into the net?

NICK:

When you make contact with the ball, you go down. Keep the racquet on a level with the ball and hit through it, not down. Remember to keep that wrist firm so you don't spray the shots.

BILLY:

Do I ever use my wrist?

NICK:

Not during the development stage. Just remember to keep the elbows away from the body, and to open the racquet face just a little for low balls.

BILLY:

I hit so many volleys off-center.

NICK:

That's because you aren't watching the ball all the way onto your racquet face. Try getting your head down just a little bit, so that it's almost behind your racquet face. It's like aiming a gun.

BILLY:

Now I'm getting it. That's better. You really have to watch the ball with this shot, don't you? When can I take a swing at the ball the way that Carling Bassett does?

NICK:

Very few players can execute a swinging volley like Carling. But when you get a floater that gives you a lot of time, you can take a little bit of a swing to knock it off and put it away. Remember, it is very important to eliminate any errors at the net. You must practice very hard.

As young players progress, they should accumulate additional tips on net play, including the importance of hitting a first volley after a serve and of picking up the half-volley, the shot that bounces at their feet. Both shots are alike in one important characteristic: in following a serve or approach shot to the net, the player must come to a stop before hitting a first volley or half-volley. Control is very important for both shots, and the wrist must be kept firm. On the half-volley, it's important to bend the knees, to get down to the ball and play it as if it were a half-groundstroke. Short backswing and follow-through. A smooth, fluid motion.

This may be a lot of instruction for a young player to digest, but these years are the learning phase, and after a time it all will become very natural. That is what you, whether coach or player, are trying to do right now—build a strong foundation. So, you young juniors, get as much out of each practice session as you can. Work with a purpose in mind. And in your tournaments, develop a positive attitude. There is joy in every victory, but learn to gain something from your losses as well. Keep a positive attitude. You are only beginning.

CODE OF CONDUCT, USTA

The highest type of sportsmanship is expected from every player! Players are under an obligation to avoid acts which are unsportsmanlike or detrimental to the game of tennis. In USTA sanctioned tournaments, violators of this code are subject to disciplinary action.

1. Loud, abusive, or profane language, racquet throwing, or hitting balls indiscriminately is prohibited.
2. Do not stall. The Rules of Tennis allow a maximum of 1½ minutes for changing ends of court on odd games and 30 seconds between points and between games when there is no changeover.
3. Intentional waving of a racquet or arms or making distracting noises is prohibited.
4. Coaching, except during the break between the second and third sets, is prohibited. (Spectators, including parents, friends and coaches, should not interfere with or participate in on-court matters.)
5. Do not attempt to make a mockery of a match, whether winning or losing.
6. Do not withdraw from a tournament after the draw has been made or default in a tournament (whether during the course of a match or prior to its commencement) except for illness, injury or personal emergency.

Tennis Etiquette

1. Wait until a point is over before walking behind a court where a match is in progress.
2. To retrieve a ball from another court or to return a ball to another court, wait until the players have completed a point.
3. Players should present a neat appearance and abide by local dress regulations.

On-Court Rules*

- If you have any doubt as to whether a ball is out or good, you must give your opponent the benefit of the doubt and play the ball as good. You should *not* play a let.
- It is your obligation to call all balls on your side, to help your opponent make calls when the opponent requests it, and to *call against yourself* (with the exception of a first service) any ball that you clearly see out on your opponent's side of the net.
- Any "out" or "let" call must be made instantaneously (i.e., made before either an opponent has hit the return or the return has gone out of play); otherwise, the ball continues in play.
- Do *not* enlist the aid of spectators in making line calls.
- If you call a ball out and then realize it was good, you should correct your call.
- To avoid controversy over the score, the Server should announce the set score (e.g., 5–4) before starting a game and the game score (e.g., 30-40) prior to serving each point.
- If players cannot agree on the score, they may go back to the last score on which there was agreement and resume play from that point, or they may spin a racquet.
- Foot faults are not allowed. If an opponent persists in foot faulting after being warned not to do so, the Referee should be informed.
- Do not stall, sulk, complain, or practice gamesmanship.

*Excerpted from the official USTA publication, "The Code," whose principles and guidelines shall apply in any match conducted without officials. Reprinted with permission of the United States Tennis Association. Additional copies are available from the USTA Education and Research Center, 729 Alexander Road, Princeton, N.J. 08540.

TIME OUT: The Little Things

What makes a champion? The same approach used to construct a Rolls-Royce: attention to small details, the little things that add up to quality. You can never be too well-organized in tennis. You can never pay too much attention to detail. "Always a little extra" is a hard-and-fast rule that will serve you well, whether it means hitting a few more minutes on your forehand, running an additional mile, or doing 10 situps over your quota.

A lot of little things go into producing a junior champion, tiny things perhaps, but they are important. For instance: Should you compete in your own age group, or (especially if you have a high ranking) should you "play up," participating in an older age division? How do you scout an opponent, looking for strengths and weaknesses? Should your tournament matches be charted? And what about coaching on the sidelines?

Here are some of my thoughts.

Age Group Competition: Everyone has individual attributes and needs, but generally speaking I think it is important to stay within your age group. This can be difficult, given the tremendous pressure to win when you are playing someone you are expected to beat. Every superstar knows that the heaviest burden can be one's own reputation. Some kids, however, simply find the pressure of their age group too much. They are big winners early in their junior careers, and then the problem of defending a position rather than attacking it begins to overwhelm them. For these players, I think an exception must be allowed. To relieve that pressure, they should play out of their age group. Some people will say this is a mistake, that these kids are simply ducking the inevitable future when they will *have* to endure that pressure. True, the day of reckoning comes to everyone. But it can come later, when the child is older and more mature, able to handle stress more easily. What we are striving for now is a way for them to improve and perform at their maximum. If they are playing not to lose, rather than playing to win, there's a danger that they will not develop their games offensively.

Of course, some kids are not overwhelmed by the strain of playing against their peers. They enjoy winning. For these players, I think staying within their own age group is wonderful. Give them a chance to learn how great winning can be. Don't deprive them of that. They will grow up soon enough.

Changing a Bad Attitude: I've already said that the way to improve in this game is to fight through the down spots, to keep trying, to keep banging on the door until it opens and you can wedge your way through. No player improves at a consistent pace. Every player goes through a slump. Every kid reaches the point where he or she gets discouraged and fed up.

Occasionally, I will be at a tournament and see one of my students put on a poor performance. I can tell that the player's heart is not in it. He (or she) has one foot out the window, ready to bail out. When this happens, I change from the gruff old coach with a soft heart into the gruff old coach with no heart. As the player comes off the court and approaches me, already beginning to whine about "bad luck" or how badly he played, I cut him short and tell him, "I'm not walking anywhere with you."

This sets him back. He says, "What? Whaddaya mean?"

"I mean I'm not walking with a loser. I want to walk with winners, a winner whether you win or lose, somebody who tried from wire to wire, not someone who gives up. Get out of here."

Sure, it's a cold way to act. But this is a time for drastic action. And what's the risk? If the kid quits tennis now, it doesn't matter, because, figuratively speaking, by not trying, he's already quit.

There is another last-ditch method a coach can use when things get bad. Earlier I talked about how important it is to stick with your game plan, to build your foundation, and not to keep changing your strokes, your playing style, or your equipment. Sometimes, however, a change is necessary. Switching racquets can be very helpful. Just keep in mind that this is your ace in the hole, and once played, its effectiveness is gone.

In March 1984, Carling Bassett switched from a Prince "Woodie" to a Prince graphite racquet, and immediately her zest for tennis was rekindled. She was like a cat on the court, eager to pounce on those volleys. "Can you believe it?" she screeched as we worked out, looking over at the spectators on the sidelines, drawing her shoulders up around her ears and mugging a big, open-mouthed grin. The racquet was giving her a new "feel." Clearly, she had grown tired of the old one.

In some cases, switching racquets can lead to disaster. Don't switch just to switch, and if you are playing well, be *very* careful. Both Sammy Giammalva and Chip Hooper, two young players on the pro circuit, went through periods of losing that coincided with changes in racquet manufacturers. Of course, they were paid large sums of money to make the switches. Money may or may not be the root of all evil, but for Sammy and Chip you could sure say it was an evil tempter.

Sizing up Opponents: Generally speaking, the best game plan is to play your own style and worry as little as possible about what is happening across the net. Of course, having said that, I must add that I tell all of my students that whenever they can, they should scout their opponents and learn what to expect from them. Football teams spend huge sums of money trying to diagnose the "tendencies" of the opposition. You would be surprised at how often such tendencies—especially weaknesses when reacting under pressure—show up in a tennis player. A few years ago, Jimmy Connors got a big boost during a match with Bjorn Borg when Pancho Segura, his coach at the time, noticed that Borg was hitting all of his passing shots down the line. Segura told Connors to cover the line, and from then on the match was his.

Let's say, for example, your opponent uses a Continental grip and for the most part is not exceptionally strong. He may be fairly solid with the forehand when in position, but will have trouble hitting crosscourt when he is forced to run wide or when the ball gets behind him. If you come to the net behind your shot, you can probably anticipate an up-the-line return because the Continental grip with the hand positioned on top of the racquet provides your opponent with less strength and causes him problems when in trouble.

Some players fight hardest when they're behind. Torben Ulrich, the eccentric Dane who was a thoughtful competitor on the pro circuit 25 years ago, once said of Manuel Santana, "It is very dangerous to lead him forty–love. It is better to lead him thirty–love, or thirty–fifteen. Forty–love is very dangerous." Ulrich's point was that Santana buckled down more the further behind he was. With opponents such as Santana, you should never take anything for granted. You must concentrate on every point—in fact, on every stroke. Always be prepared for the ball to come back, no matter how far out of position your opponent is. Keep putting away the ball. In the end, even the fiercest fighter will cave in.

At the other end of the spectrum is the player who is best with the lead. Ivan Lendl has a reputation as a front-runner who will blast you off the court once he has the edge. He has an "I came, I saw, I conquered" style. With this kind of opponent it is imperative to win the first game, to stay at least even early in the match. Don't coast along, expecting to make up ground later. Play each early point as if it were match point, because in effect it is.

When you scout opponents, don't simply look to see which is the player's better side, the forehand or the backhand. Make a mental note to ascertain what he does in certain situations. Does he attack when behind? Does he serve and volley on break point? Does he let the overheads bounce in crucial situations? Does he attack weak second serves? Watch and learn.

Charting Your Mistakes: This is something that goes right along with the above. Some players are always berating this or that part of their game. "My forehand is the pits," they yell.

The Academy's Broadway and 42nd Street.

Or, "I can't serve." They are not only alibiing, they are often completely wrong. They would be surprised to discover how wrong.

A good way to diagnose the strengths and weaknesses of your game is to have someone chart your matches. Using this method, we saw that Jimmy Arias in his early years made far too many forehand errors when he was pinned behind the baseline. We showed him that he had to be a bit more patient with this shot and not try for an impossible winner; instead, he should clear the net with more topspin and depth, and wait for a better attacking opportunity.

Charting a match might show that you are getting killed with your second serve, that your opponent is attacking nine out of 10 times off a "pushed" service. The solution, of course, is to put a little more spin on your first serve and get it in more frequently.

Charting also can reveal weaknesses in concentration. If you were ahead in almost every game and still lost the match, you were obviously suffering such lapses.

When keeping a chart, concentrate on three types of points: unforced errors (note on what shots they occurred), key points (who won them and how), and winners (note the game scores and how they occurred).

I learned the importance of both scouting and charting back when I was coaching junior tennis in Springfield, Ohio—in those days the scene of one of the nation's biggest tournaments, the Western Junior Championships. All of the top juniors—Arthur Ashe, Stan Smith, Dennis Ralston, Brian Gottfried—showed up, but the fellow I remember clearly was Bill Lenoir, a fine clay-court performer, quiet and reserved. He always carried a little notebook with him. One day I asked him about it and he showed it to me. It was a diary with brief descriptions of almost every top junior player in the United States. For instance, under "Clark Graebner" he had written: "Big serve, tough volleys, solid ground-strokes, lets little things bother him on the court. Try and wear him down mentally." These were the little "keys" Lenoir had studied and was thinking about when he took the court against an opponent. In tennis, you have to know yourself, but it also helps to know your opponent.

Coaching on the Sidelines: An anachronism of tennis is the rule against coaching on the sidelines. Everyone does it. No one does anything about it. Where's the beef? Usually on the pages of newspapers and magazines. All tennis writers know that if they are stuck for a column, they can always write about sideline coaching. One week they can deplore it as a horrible offense that gives a player an unfair advantage, and the next they can say that it is a reality of the game whose time has come.

Okay, all you purists out there, hold onto your school ties and blazers, I'm going to admit it: There are times when I coach from the sidelines! As does almost every other coach who is worth a tennis lesson. Anyone who puts his or her heart and soul into the game of tennis will find it hard to resist the temptation to help out a "student in need" with a timely nod or word of encouragement.

Of course, verbal commands are harder to deny. I'll always cherish the advice Australian Lew Hoad yelled to his wife, Jenny, when she was playing a tournament in England. Hoad wanted her to take advantage of an opponent who had trouble moving up and back on the court. Shouted Lew, "One short, and one long, stupid." Now, some people might say Hoad's advice was an obvious example of coaching. I prefer to point out that in its form of address it more likely qualifies as an oral suicide note. After that little coaching excess, Lew probably needed someone to taste Jenny's cooking for him over the next couple of weeks.

One advantage of a reputation for coaching from the sidelines is that your player's opponent often ends up worrying more about what you may or may not be doing than what your player is doing. It's like being a spitball pitcher and having the batters complain to the umpire because they think you are greasing up every pitch, when really all you are doing is scratching your head. At the French Open in 1982, Andrea Jaeger complained bitterly after a defeat to Martina Navratilova that Martina's coach, Renee Richards, was making like one of those semaphores used by the Navy to signal between ships. Probably Andrea's concentration was bothered more by the thought that someone was violating the rules at her expense than by the signals themselves.

An obvious solution would be to make sideline coaching legal. Every other sport has it. What is so different about tennis? When people ask me why there is no coaching allowed (except in team competitions, such as the Davis Cup), I shrug my shoulders—the same reaction I once had when people asked me why tennis players wore white clothing. "It's tradition," I say.

11

FOUR BIG YEARS (Twelve to Sixteen)

At 12 years of age, it's time for you to develop the disciplines and rules that will enable you to progress right up the ladder of greatness. I'm a firm believer in rules. At the Academy, none of the students smoke cigarettes. They would not be so inane as to put so much hard work into their physical well-being and then defeat that work by smoking. But the "No Smoking" signs around the Academy grounds are not for the students—they're for the people who visit. Some of them are taken aback by the signs. After all, they're outsiders—what's the harm of smoking?

"No," my assistant will say. "There's too much danger of something catching on fire."

The visitor will look around at the grass, the trees, the shrubs and flowers. "What could possibly catch on fire?" they will ask.

"Nick will," says my assistant. "If Nick sees you smoking, there will be a big explosion."

We have other rules, other little disciplines. For instance, no one driving an Academy automobile is allowed to use the radio. These cars are one of our sponsors' gifts to the Academy. I don't want them destroyed in a wreck because someone's attention was diverted. A petty rule, you might say, like no gum chewing, no talking during drills, and no extracurricular television—but it's all part of our code of discipline at the Academy.

Here's another way to get under my skin. I hate it when a parent brings me an already-developed player and the parent says, "They've got the talent, they just need someone to draw it out of them." I can see the player is an "80-percenter." She's lazy. Her strokes are great—*pa-pa-pow*—but she stands up too straight. Why? Because it's easier not to bend. She lets the short balls bounce twice before she hits them. If she hits a ball off-center, right away she looks at her racquet, as if it has betrayed her. She gets a short ball and she goes for a showy shot—what basketball coach Al McGuire calls "French pastry"—and blasts the ball into the back fence. Even in this short little workout, her concentration wavers.

Eighty-percenters. I don't want them. Sure, they've had a few years of instruction and now they want to get serious about tennis, now they want to go to work. Hey, their time card has been canceled. They didn't punch it when it was valid, when they had the chance to commit themselves to the program. Turn out the lights, the party's over.

The years between 12 and 16 are the most important years of a tennis player's life. These are the years when you will progress. Do you have the resolve to do it? Can you make a sacrifice? For four years? Can you dedicate yourself so that *every day* is a building block that fits perfectly into the day that preceded it?

I'll tell you the answer. The answer is no. It's an impossible goal. No one ever has done it. People come close, but no one can be perfect. You will have days when things do not go right. You will be sick. Hey, there probably will be days when you goof off. But fight, fight, fight. Remember: four years. You trade four years for a lifetime. Is that too much to ask?

I criticize, but I criticize with a purpose. With some kids, it seems as if the god of discovery is always against them. They do something wrong, they always get caught. One of my students is Kevin Arias, the 12-year-old brother of Jimmy. The other day, just as I walked around a corner, he was stuffing a cookie in his mouth. "You eating cookies again?" I yelled. Kevin had crumbs all over his face. He looked like a cat with canary feathers sticking out of his mouth.

Another time I was looking out my window. We have a rule that says the kids are not allowed to cut across the grass, and to help them remember there are ropes up—it being harder to lift the ropes and climb through than to walk the few extra feet around, using the proper walkway. So what did I see when I looked out my window but Kevin Arias, climbing through the ropes. I couldn't believe it. Of course, I had to tell him about it. But I waited for the right time. I didn't go out there ranting and raving. I know too much criticism can break a kid's spirit. What I did was wait until late that afternoon, when Kevin was scheduled to work with me in a practice session. I knew that little Kevin would be tired. It's the end of a long, long day. He's had school, he's had the group drills, he's had his running and aerobics, he's worked out on Nautilus. All of this work, he's done day after day for months. He's probably sick of it. Now he's going to practice with me watching him.

"You're always in trouble, aren't you?" I told him as we began our session.

Kevin looked at me kind of funny. "What's Nick talking about?" he was thinking to himself.

"Today, I look out my window and who do I see cutting through the grass? You, Kevin. I see you."

Now Kevin looked a little fidgety. Now he had to redeem himself. *Pa-pa-pow.*

I wish you could see this kid hit a ball. It just flies across the net. He's 12 years old and about as tall as a barrel, but his backhand is about 20 years old. His forehand is about 25. He's a great kid.

Later in our workout, Kevin hit a sliced backhand. Now, Kevin has a wonderful topspin backhand, much better, in fact, than even the one his brother, Jimmy, had at the same age. But on this shot, Kevin just had to throw in a little French pastry.

I went nuts. "Give me twenty," I yelled. Kevin looked at me. "Give me twenty squat jumps right now! No sliced back- hands. You know better than that." Kevin stepped aside and did 20 squat jumps, a little smile on his face.

Later, when he was back on the baseline, he ran for a ball and, not thinking, started to hit a sliced backhand. In mid- stroke he caught himself and stopped. "That doesn't count," Kevin yelled. "I stopped."

Boy, I liked that.

This is the type of lesson that is so important to children as they enter the next phase of their development. They've got the tools, the basics. They've learned their strokes. Now they have to learn how to put them to use.

There's another thing that drives me wild. A player goes to a tournament. Maybe this player has perfect strokes. He hits the ball wonderfully. But he loses the tournament. I ask my assistant why. My assistant looks at me. Then he shrugs his shoulders and taps the side of his head with his forefinger. "He played dumb," he says.

"What," I'll yell. "Whaaaat?" I sound as distraught as a farmer who has just checked his fields and found worms in the corn. Pretty strokes mean nothing. I want my kids to go to a tournament and to play one level better there. And on the big points, I want them to play *another* level better.

Jimmy Arias has always been a tournament player. On a backcourt at the Academy, with no one watching, he can be "cake," an easy mark. A lot of kids can beat him. But put him on the no. 1 court, with people watching, and he becomes a different player.

The difference between no. 1 and no. 200 on the pro circuit is almost infinitesimal. Yet the lower-ranked players will be pressed to win even one game from the champion; they always seem to be one stroke behind in the rallies. The Bjorn Borg–Ivan Lendl match in the 1981 finals of the French Open provided a fine example of how you break down an opponent. Lendl had played Borg dead even for four sets, but in the fifth set, you could see Borg's resolve grow. He simply dug in on the baseline, hitting every ball back, refusing to make a mistake, refusing to allow a shot go by him. Finally, at the end, Lendl grew weary. He had fought and fought and fought but finally he got tired of punching. Borg was like one of those air-filled punching bags weighted on the bottom so that when you hit them they topple, then spring back. Borg kept rebounding. Final set score, 6–1. Championship to Borg on a technical knockout.

From where does that resolve come? I say it comes from dedication and concentration instilled in you as a child. When Brian Gottfried was a kid, he would climb the fence around the tennis courts at night and practice his serve by moonlight. But hey, I've had students who did not want to work. I've had students who could not see where it was going to lead them, who did not want a chance to be champion. For every winner, there are countless losers.

Great strokes are not enough. Saying you are a tennis player because you have all the shots is like saying you are a race car driver because you have just bought a Ferrari. You've got the equipment, that's all.

Years ago I was in a supermarket with a friend. There was another shopper there, a guy about 25 years old. He was carrying a New York Knicks gym bag. My friend pointed at him, recognizing the fellow as someone who had led the country in scoring as a college sophomore.

"See that guy?" he asked me. "He had a 'can't miss' tag. Except for one thing—he missed."

Don't get to believing that you're a "can't miss" player. As you progress through these four years, always remember that there is someone better. Don't think you are so good that you can't improve. Keep working.

Now is the time to learn some valuable lessons that will take you far. It is important that you develop good habits. Two of the most important things in tennis are learning from your mistakes and exploiting an opponent's weakness. They go together like bread and butter.

When you make a mistake, your first reaction should be: Why? Likewise, when your opponent makes a mistake, it's your responsibility to gauge the reason it happened. I've had students who refused to think, who refused *to catalogue knowledge.* I make a correction in their groundstrokes. The next ball comes, they hit it perfectly. The next ball comes, they go back to the incorrect way of hitting the ball. Why? Very simple—they can't remember what I told them 15 seconds ago. The same thing happens to them in matches. They lose. People on the sidelines point to their foreheads and tap with their fingers.

Service drill at the Academy.

Serving while on your knees develops the ability to hit up into the ball.

In addition to cataloging knowledge, now is the time you should go big on those earlier-noted weapons in your game. One of the best, and one used very effectively by Jimmy Arias, Mats Wilander, Bjorn Borg, and Ivan Lendl, is the runaround forehand. The Old School used to preach over and over that a player should never run around a backhand in order to hit a forehand. The reasoning was twofold: first, it hindered the development of a player's backhand through disuse; second, it forced the player to take an extra step or two, and it opened up a side of the court for his opponent.

What the new players, such as Jimmy Arias, who favor the game of Power Tennis have discovered is that running around the backhand can have several *advantages*. Now they can hit a powerful offensive stroke, either down the line or crosscourt, using an inside-out stroke to their opponent's backhand side. Let's say you take the second option, hitting the inside-out shot to X's backhand. Sure, now the down-the-line backhand is open for X, and you must recover from the runaround forehand and cover the open court to your right. But by the same token, X, under pressure, must hit the down-the-line backhand, one of the most difficult shots in tennis. And if X does not hit it perfectly, you have an easy forehand to a wide-open court. *Pa-pa-pow.* The point's over.

The key element of Power Tennis is, of course, fitness, and these are the years for all-out training and physical development. Jimmy Arias, along with other proponents of the runaround forehand, have to be in tremendous shape to be able to consistently hit the shot and recover in time to cover the open court. This also has another important advantage in the runaround forehand. By covering the open court, the Power Player frustrates the opponent. Now X will try to hit backhand crosscourt, striving to make his tormentor hit a backhand rather than the more-powerful runaround forehand. This puts tremendous pressure on X, and often results in errors when X hits the ball wide, or long. The runaround forehand can be a simple but very effective weapon that allows you to dictate the match.

There are several key elements to setting up the shot. First, it is important that you keep your opponent off-balance during the rallies by mixing up your shot selection. Hit deep balls to your adversary's weaker stroke. Throw in some high floaters and occasionally hit a few drop shots. Then when your opponent hits a weak or a short return, run around your

Jimmy Arias's power forehand, his big offensive weapon.

backhand and tee off with a big offensive forehand. It's not necessary to hit a clean winner, but be ready to come to the net to finish the point off with a volley, or to cover the open court if your opponent is in position for a good return.

Here's a typical lesson from the Academy that demonstrates how you set up the shot.

NICK:

Don, today I want to practice shots, concentrating on being consistent and accurate. Try to make your shots deep, to have them land three feet inside the baseline. Remember: Watch the ball. Prepare quickly. Get your racquet head low, and hit up and through the ball. Follow through, and keep your feet moving to get into position.

DON:

Nick, I noticed when I hit the ball real deep to you, some of your returns come back very shallow.

NICK:

You're right. You have put me under pressure with your deep shots. Now let's do something more with the ball when I hit a short one. I'll feed you balls about ten feet inside your baseline. They won't be hit hard, but no matter where they land, I want you to hit your forehand.

DON:

Do you want me to run around my backhand and hit all my forehands for winners?

NICK:

Don, even for Jimmy Arias, that's impossible. Remember: When you run around your backhand, you're leaving a lot of open court. So your shot has to be offensive and well-placed. The part of the court you're in will help determine if you go for an outright winner. In any case, be ready to come to the net to cut off the short return.

Geoffrey Marks's topspin backhand, another powerful offensive stroke.

DON [later]:

Nick, we've hit about fifty balls so far, but I'm still not confident running around and hitting my forehand. It feels like I'm leaving too much open court.

NICK:

That's a natural reaction, Don. You're trying something new. Remember, practice will make it better. Let's hit another hundred balls, only hit them a little harder and deeper than the last ones. Hit all forehands. Remember, you have got to move your feet quickly to take advantage of that short ball. To hit with confidence you have to take the offensive and make sure to hit the ball above waist level if possible. Get into position every time—this is an offensive shot. This time, after you hit your shot, move to the net to take the volley. You're really looking more confident now. See how you're hitting the ball at waist level or above, and hitting from a low-to-high position with topspin? You must really POP the ball, accelerating the racquet head. What you are doing is driving nails into your opponent's coffin with this shot, Don. That's good. Now you're making an offensive shot that will force your opponent into errors and a weak return. That's what the runaround forehand is all about.

At the Academy we drill every day on the runaround forehand. A pro feeds short balls to the students. Maybe I am standing behind them, hunched over, watching closely, like a cat about to spring. The students must hit big offensive shots for winners. This teaches them to go for the winner when they have a setup opening. Nothing drives me as crazy as seeing a student set up an opportunity for a winner, and then hit a less-than-powerful shot that the opponent is able to run down. It's like writing a letter and never mailing it. Now the opponent is back into the point, and worse, he has a psychological edge because he knows that he can reach your best shots and that you are hesitant to take advantage of your opportunities.

The difference between being a good player and being a great player can be just that—hesitating when you have the opening. You must go for the winner. Put the ball away.

The one thing I have tried to make clear throughout this chapter is: Do not let yourself become the player who has the talent but never reaches your true potential. Don't leave a stream of people tapping their heads in the wake of your defeats. Work hard. Work harder. Work the hardest of anyone you know. Four years . . . maybe to greatness. Is that too much to ask?

12

TIME OUT:
Fighters

At the end of the last chapter I started getting into a quality you hear about so often in tennis: the will to fight. What I'm talking about is never giving up, no matter how hopeless the cause. Many matches have been won by underdogs who were behind 6–0, 5–0. Anything can happen. Your opponent can suffer an injury. Or become ill. The point is that you must *learn* to fight, especially when you are behind. Ivan Lendl, who lost to Jimmy Connors in the finals of the 1983 U.S. Open, tarnished his reputation terribly that day because, rightly or wrongly, onlookers perceived that he gave less than a wholehearted effort after he fell behind. What people believe, however, is irrelevant. It's the player who counts.

The difference between winners and losers often comes down to determination, to scrappiness and resolve. These must be a major part of your four-year development program; they must become as much a part of your arsenal as your forehand or backhand. Jimmy Arias has always been supremely confident on the court—cocky, some might say. I like that. It's cocky players who don't cave in when they find themselves in a pressure situation. The confident player loves the pressure, thrives on it. Early in his career, Arias played Jimmy Connors, who knows a thing or two about cockiness. At one juncture in the match, Arias hit a volley for a winner, and yelled out, "Yeah!" Connors called him to the net. "Settle down, young fellow," he said. "Settle down." Arias looked at him, then walked back to the service line and cranked out an ace. "How's that for settling down?" he called over to Connors. Was that cockiness? I say it's being a fighter, backing up yourself with action.

Martina Navratilova is at the top of her game right now, the undisputed queen of tennis. But she had to get mentally tough to reach her goal. She had all the shots—an amazing repertoire, in fact—but she lost one big match after another until Nancy Lieberman straightened her out. Lieberman knows all about the athlete's psyche because of her remarkable motivation as a top basketball player. She saw that Martina had to develop strength that went outside of her groundstrokes. Martina learned Lieberman's lessons well and in 1982 and 1983 she compiled the greatest record in the history of women's tennis.

Now that you are 14 or 15 and you have been involved in junior tennis for a few years, perhaps you are a little unhappy with the way things are going. It could be that your ranking is not what you want it to be, or your game has not developed the way you thought it would. I say: Don't give up. Not only can you turn it around, you can turn it around in a big way. Greg Holmes, who came out of Utah University to win the 1983 NCAA championships and then went on to defeat Guillermo Vilas in the U.S. Open the same year, never was a highly ranked player in the juniors. But his game came together during college. He kept at it, kept working. He was a fighter.

I know something about comebacks in life. I've been up, and I've been down. In fact, only a few short years ago, before I started the Academy, most tennis people regarded me as a failure, the Edsel of the sport. In 1975, after a summer of giving clinics throughout the country, I returned to my New York office to check on how my three tennis camps were going. The word was not so good. To my utter amazement, I found that I was $122,000 in debt. As a result I lost everything but a typewriter, the only piece of office furniture that remained after the bill collectors carried everything else off. A typewriter—and I didn't even type!

It is funny now. The debts have been paid off. In fact, those red numbers seem miniscule compared with the black figures we now deal with. My point is, don't ever think that you can get too far behind to come back.

My friends kid me sometimes. They say that I can make a dead weed grow flowers, that I will stand over it and fertilize it, and water it, and beg it until the darn thing comes to life. All I know is this: If you stay the task, the job gets easier.

How did the Academy get going again? Jimmy Arias, Kathleen Horvath, and Carling Bassett were the three kids I

Kathleen Horvath and Jimmy
Arias, circa 1978—two of
Nick's first champions.

picked to stay in my house at the time. I saw to it that they,
like me, never had an off day. But they made it, and the
Academy made it with them. All of them, still teenagers, are
out on the pro tours and doing well. I don't care how much
talent they had. I challenge anybody to take three kids, aged
10 to 13, and turn them into champions. That's what we
did—and not only into champions. We turned them into
fighters.

I've already said some things about concentration. You
need more and more of it the further you develop your game.
The other day Eric Korita, another of my students who is on the

pro tour, gave me the greatest compliment I ever hope to get when he told my assistant, Gabe Jaramillo, "Nick's like magic. He comes around and I start to play better." Now if only I could make Eric see the reason why. It's because of concentration, the same kind of concentration you need in your matches. When Eric sees me watching him, he starts thinking better, and that makes him a better player.

So those are two of the things you need to work on now—being a fighter and concentration. You also need to check your game and make certain that you are developing an all-court attack. How's your serve and volley? Can you play consistently from the baseline?

In the next few years you are going to mature. Your body will change. Maybe you are small now, but you're lithe and quick. Your tendency is to try to be a baseliner. But what

The first volley drill: put-away at the net.

happens if you suddenly sprout several inches and add a lot of weight? Then your mobility will be threatened, and because you have neglected your serve and your net game, you will be at a tremendous disadvantage. The same thing can happen in reverse. You can be considered big for your age and feel you can win only with a Power Game, but in a few years the other players might well be big as you, maybe bigger. Keep working on *all* facets of the game.

One way to do this is to break down tennis into small components. Everyone practices a backhand and a forehand, and most people work on overheads and volleys. But few people are specific enough. Rarely, for instance, does anyone practice the little nuances such as the half-volley or the first volley—shots you'll have to hit if you ever hope to win points with your serve in top competition, shots that are essential to your arsenal as a fighter.

With this in mind, I am going to give you a first-volley lesson that comes straight from the practice courts at the Academy. Remember when practicing the first volley that depth and placement are two key elements. You are trying not so much to put away the ball as to force your opponent into a weak return you can knock off for a winner as you close to the net. The important elements of first-volley technique include: meeting the ball far out in front (which helps you eliminate your backswing); slowing down and stopping so that you can control your body as you hit the shot; making a slight shoulder turn that allows you to step toward the net as you meet the ball; and maintaining a firm wrist, hitting through the ball with control.

NICK:
Let's keep score in our lesson today. We'll serve and volley.

LOUIS [losing serve]:
You were lucky to win that point.

NICK:
Perhaps, but you hit a very poor first volley. You ran through the volley! This is absolutely the worst mistake you can make with the shot. It takes you from an offensive to a defensive position. Likely as not, it will cause you to hit a weak volley and allow your opponent to jump all over it. By stopping, you are able to control the shot. Zero–fifteen.

LOUIS [losing another]:
Look at that. Another good serve and volley and still you passed me.

NICK:

Just because you hit it hard does not make it a good first volley. You must hit it deep, with good direction. That will make it difficult for me to hit an offensive shot. Your volley landed on the service line. Zero–thirty.

LOUIS:

Okay. Get ready. [Loses another.]

NICK:

Zero–forty. You went for an outright winner, and wound up hitting the ball over the baseline. This is a low-percentage shot unless you are capable of moving in very close to the net—like someone with great speed, say, Vitas Gerulaitis.

LOUIS [finally wins point]:

That time I did it. I concentrated on the ball and thought of the target area we worked on. Fifteen–forty.

NICK:

Keep in mind, Louis, that at fifteen–forty, the server still has control of the game. In fact, even though you are behind in score, most people would say that a good server would have the advantage. They forget, however, that the server also must be a very good volleyer. Now you must dig in to pull yourself out of the hole. Make certain that you get your first serve in.

LOUIS:

One question. I feel like going for more direct winners and even trying some short angle-volleys.

NICK:

This isn't the time for that. You're down in the game, not ahead. Try to think of yourself as a gambler. Strive to put the odds in your favor. Your first volley should be hit to the portion of the court that you are able to see above the net. Anything more daring means trouble. To see more of the court, learn to close to the net sooner. Above all, learn to be patient with your volleys. Don't go for the flashy shot, especially when you are behind in a game.

LOUIS [another winner]:

Thirty–forty. I see. I hit my volley down the line, as you told me.

NICK:

That's right. Hit the majority of your first volleys down the line, follow the correct angle into the net and you will come out ahead.

LOUIS:

I'm after you now.

NICK:

Fault. Second service. My game! Louis, don't ease up on your second serve. You gave me too much time to run around my backhand to tee off on a big forehand. I warned you about failing to get your first serve in, but having failed, you must concentrate on a good second serve. Don't let up, even on game point. It is like being a basketball player and passing up open shots. Pretty soon, your opponent will not even guard you. Your second serve must make your opponent think defense. If you allow him to attack your second serve, you're finished.

LOUIS:
Let's practice first volleys. I feel about ready to make the breakthrough.

NICK:
Try positioning yourself in the vicinity of the service line. I'll stand about three feet inside the baseline. Let's volley back and forth. Half-volleys don't count when hit to me. This drill will force you to hit through the volleys, gaining depth and accuracy. Remember, this is a control shot.

LOUIS:
I do fairly well on my first volleys above the net, but the low ones cause trouble.

NICK:
Moving in faster will allow you to hit the ball when it's higher. But sometimes good returns will leave the ball at your feet. Concentrate on bending the front knee, getting down to the level of the ball, and keeping a firm wrist. When you are down low, open your racquet face slightly on contact for a little underspin. This will help your control and help lift the ball for depth.

Back-fence volley drill.

LOUIS:
This is a good lesson, but is there any specific exercise to help me cut down my backswing?

NICK:
Come over to my side of the court. I'm going to give you a surefire way to stop that extra motion. Get right up against the back fence. Place your back against it. Now we will volley back and forth.

LOUIS:
That's not fair. I can't take my racquet back without hitting the fence.

NICK:
Right. That's the idea. Too big a swing gets you into trouble. The fence forces you to take a very small backswing. Practice against the fence every day and you'll develop the perfect stroke for the first volley. Remember, don't wait for the ball to come to you. Get it out in front. Stay in control.

A strong net game can be a very effective way both to exert and to combat pressure. If you can serve and volley and win points, you are in control of the match. By holding your service every time, you put extreme pressure on your opponents when they are serving. They know that if they are broken they will be in big trouble.

Pressure is a little-understood factor in a match. Certain points in each contest are much more important than others. Learn to play the big points well (we'll identify them shortly) and you will learn to win. I think it's important to practice just as you play. Take a lesson from other sports such as football, which has a two-minute drill, and set up situations that you might face when you are playing. For instance, practice returning serve when you are at deuce. Play the point as if it were your or your opponent's ad.

Remember the importance of maintaining deep breathing. Once again, learn from another sport. Basketball coaches teach their players that when attempting foul shots, they must take a deep breath just before shooting the ball.

As you prepare to return serve, conjure up a mental image of winning the point, taking the serve and returning it hard. Then take a slight step forward as the server contacts the ball. This forces you to move into the shot and lets you capitalize on your opponent's power by catching the ball on the rise.

Arthur Ashe, when he surprised a lot of people by winning Wimbledon in 1975 at the age of 32, sat staring into a towel during the changeovers. Later he said he was trying to project a positive image of his game. He called it "being in the zone," a phrase that soon became popular in tennis. Ashe was talking about letting your mind concentrate only on tennis during a match, with no outside distractions. But more, he also meant thinking positively so that when you went for a difficult shot, your body took over and produced marvelous results.

What are the crucial points in a match? Someone once said that crucial points are any points that you lose, but that is too easy an explanation. Generally speaking, the fourth point of every game is the crucial point to win. Usually this point either allows one player to go up 40–15 or ties the game at deuce. If you can always win the fourth point, you will do very well.

Another crucial point is the first, the one that leads off the game. Even Roscoe Tanner, who had the most imposing serve in pro tennis for a decade, seemed a bit unnerved whenever he lost the first point while serving. Opposing players got quite a lift when they noticed this.

When receiving serve, go for a big return to open the game. It can turn around the game for you. And if you make an error, you are not at that much of a disadvantage.

Any game point, obviously, is another big one. When Jimmy Arias is returning serve and has a break point, he uses a tip he picked up from John Newcombe: He shades himself over to the backhand side, daring the server to go down the middle. Arias is sending the server the message that he is going to tee off with a big forehand. This can be unsettling.

By the same token, let's say you're the server and there is a break point against you. I guarantee you that you'll be surprised how often a gutsy play will win the point for you, especially if it is not expected by your opponent. Across the net, he will be excited about an opportunity to break your serve. But if he's not a fighter like Arias, he may go for a "safe" return. If you are alert, you can jump all over it.

Deuce points also loom large in any match. Win a deuce point and you have only to win one more point to win the game. Lose it, and you'll have to win three more. Take a hint from Bjorn Borg on these points. Play coolly. Don't let yourself get upset at a bad break that sets the score at deuce. If you crack here, your opponent may well win the next two points, and the game, while you are trying to get your attitude back together. Just don't go wild. Get your first serve in. Try to force an error.

There are several other instances when certain points are larger than others. Generally speaking, the seventh game of each set has an added importance. This is especially true if the set is 3–3. Win this game at all costs.

Finally you are confronted with the biggest point of all—the last one. How to end matches is something you need to learn. The person who is behind will do anything possible to keep the match going. He will run down balls that earlier he probably wouldn't have tried for. He will lob. If you have game, set, or match point, it's usually best to go to your bread-and-butter shots. This isn't the time to try and hit a flashy winner. Execute the shot in which you have the most confidence.

Remember, fighters never give up. They play the crucial points as if their opponents were trying to take money out of their pockets. They don't choke because they always feel they can come back. They play with confidence, and they remember Nick. They go to work.

13

LARGE QUESTIONS AND EARLY REWARDS (Sixteen and Seventeen)

At age 16, you have to take a long look at yourself and where you are going in this game. You have put in a lot of hard work. Do you want to continue, maybe turn pro—if not quite yet, in another year or two? Are the rewards equal to the effort? Now is the time to make that kind of decision. Sit down with your parents and your coach and talk about it. Maybe things do not seem to be working out as well as you and your parents imagined they would when you began playing. Maybe that dream of being the world's no. 1 player seems impossibly remote. Not everyone, obviously, can be no. 1. But so what? I guarantee you that the work you have put into your tennis will be an emotional credit for you the rest of your life. Two years from now, for instance, you will be ready to begin college. Dedicate yourself for a couple of seasons more and your education could be paid for through a scholarship.

Tennis and academics go together. President John F. Kennedy once said, "Intelligence and skill can only function at the peak of their capacity when the body is healthy and strong." Tennis should not interfere with your studies, it should enhance them. If you can organize your practice time and your tournament schedule, you can organize your time for the books. My staff does this for Academy students. We have a rule: If it comes down to studying or playing a tournament, studying comes first . . . second . . . and third. Just as I believe that the more you practice, the better your game becomes, I also believe that the more you study, the better your brain becomes. And a better brain means a better game. It is no accident that so many tennis players are also excellent students.

Both endeavors require discipline, now more than ever. At the Academy, we recently had a student who was giving us a hard time. Having been in the program for several years, he was full of false bravado. He had all the answers. He *knew*. So he began skipping out on the practice drills, not doing the extra work that we like to see, neglecting his studies. The more he got away with, the more he tried to get away with. One day in the cafeteria, after I returned from a trip, several staff members mentioned the boy to me. They told me how disappointed they were. Across the way, the boy was looking at us, probably aware he was being discussed. I walked over and read him the riot act. "If you don't stay with the program, you're out of the program," I told him. "If you don't straighten up, there's the door." I really let him have it. And he straightened out.

Parents can learn something from this little incident. No matter how talented your child, don't forget that he or she is only a teenager and still needs to be disciplined. People are amazed when they discover that many of our young professionals stay with us in the normal Academy housing when they are off the circuit. We treat them like teenagers, not like world travelers.

Last year I walked out to the courts where our best students were taking part in a round-robin. Many of the Academy's younger kids were watching. The older kids were clowning around on the court, showing off, strutting their stuff. It was deplorable. "Okay," I yelled, "you guys want to put on a show, now you're going to give us all a show. Get out there on the track and start running. I want everybody out running!" One kid protested. "I have to play a tournament tomorrow," he said. I answered, "I don't care. I don't care if you lose in the first round. Get out there."

I'm never surprised when my best students try to get away with something, and parents should not be taken aback when their teenage child breaks a rule, either. It is the kid's way of testing you, of probing for a weakness, of doing the same thing that adolescents have done with their parents over the ages.

Kevin Arias, tennis player and student.

Similarly, don't be shocked at this stage if your child begins to feel uncomfortable with her tennis, even if she's been having tremendous success. The problem is not getting there—the problem is staying there. It can be harder defending a position than attacking it. Recently, Lisa Bonder came to me. Her world ranking as a professional had jumped to no. 11. Said Lisa, "I'm glad, but I'm a little scared. I wonder if I can keep it up." Self-doubt is all part of tennis, even for a professional such as Lisa. The way to ease that doubt is to work harder.

The Gyro-Jump, an Academy training tool.

A few days ago Aaron Krickstein and I had that little talk. I knew it was coming. I told him he had to rededicate himself, that he had to concentrate on his physical conditioning. A couple of afternoons later I found out he had skipped an aerobics class. I ran looking for him, and told him about it.

"Well, Jimmy Arias doesn't take aerobics," Aaron said. "Why do I have to?" As a matter of fact, Arias was not even at the Academy at the time, and if he had been, chances are he would have taken the class, or done comparable work so that he could maintain his cardiovascular conditioning. Aaron was just trying to justify his having let me down. I told him, "Listen, you're always comparing yourself to Arias. I'm talking about you, not Jimmy. God gave Jimmy feet. He gave you boats. You get the picture?"

It is only natural, especially if you're having a lot of success, to forget about some of your off-the-court training, especially foot training. Don't fall into that trap. Your feet are as important to your tennis as hands are to a pianist. It is no accident that two of the quickest players in the game today, Bjorn Borg and Vitas Gerulaitis, were excellent soccer players as young kids. They learned how to move their feet.

We've talked about agility drills. Another effective tool for helping your court movement is the Gyro-Jump (see photos). This is a new kind of jump rope with a unique construction. The handles are longer and heavier than those on a normal jump rope, so that the effort required when jumping builds your upper body as well as your legs. Robert Miller, the inventor of the Gyro-Jump, has instituted a full exercise program for our Academy students. He calls the Gyro-Jump the first improvement in the 50 years since the jump rope was first used, and I'm inclined to agree with him. Prior to playing a tournament, many of our players first warm up by using the Gyro-Jump for a couple of minutes. It's a fantastic way to loosen up your body and to ease the pressure of the upcoming match.

Now that you are 16, you must once again (as you should have done after each of the preceding three years) take the time to evaluate your game. Note your weaknesses and strengths, and refer to your training journal (see p. 70) for hints as to why or how the negative and positive aspects have evolved. What can you do to remedy your faults? Develop a new plan of practice and exercise that, hopefully, will solve the problem. For instance, if you are getting tired in the third set, you need to increase your jogging and calisthenics. Work on your groundstrokes in the same way. If you are having trouble in matches hitting a topspin passing shot under pressure, one remedy would be a drill that I have seen many professionals employ. One player stands at the baseline, the other at the net with a large bucket of balls. The player at the net feeds balls to the baseline player. But "feed" is a very inaccurate word in this case. He hits the balls at the baseline player as hard and as deep as he can. The baseliner is under tremendous pressure. Once again, this is what I mean when I advocate practicing match situations. Do this drill every day for a month and you will see a remarkable difference in your passing shots.

One stroke that most players fail to develop through practice is the approach shot. Any time you get a short ball at the service line, you should be able to come to the net behind a good, deep, accurate approach shot. Maybe you are having

Chris Garner and the approach shot.

trouble doing this. Chances are that you haven't been practicing this stroke. One key could be your technique. We know how important it is to get to the ball quickly. I believe it takes longer if you run with your racquet completely back. Instead take it back just before you get to the ball. This way the running and the backswing complement each other and this allows you the extra split second you need to control your body as you come to a stop and execute the stroke. Likely as not, you will be unable to come to a complete stop, but slow down as much as possible, drive the ball, then continue on to the net. One, two, three—each component is as important as every other. Strive for accuracy and depth. If the ball is above the net, you can hit with topspin or hit it flat—another reason to reach it quickly—before it has dropped. But if the ball is low and you are forced to hit underspin, make sure you maintain a firm wrist and a long follow-through. This keeps you from floating the ball and making yourself a sitting duck when the ball bounces high. Underspin keeps the ball low. For the most part, go down the line with this shot, except when you are trying to surprise your opponent or keep him honest. By hitting crosscourt, you leave too much of the court open. On the other hand, hitting the approach down the line and then coming in puts you in a better position to cover your opponent's return.

Handling the short balls is a key to any good player's success. Watch how the pros almost never make a mistake on a short ball, while junior players constantly mess up this shot.

The approach shot is not your only option when you get a short ball at the service line. You also are now in position for a drop shot. Only you don't have to use it; you can save it. By this I mean that early in the match, hit approach shots off short balls, then later, when you are at a key point, your opponent will not be expecting a drop shot. Don't waste opportunities for drop shots by squandering them early, taking away the element of surprise that you need to make this shot work.

One variation in court coverage after you hit a good drop shot is to follow it to the net. When your opponent reaches the ball, the weak return can be picked off at the net. However, you must be alert for the lob. Don't try this strategy unless you are accomplished at the drop shot. Through poor judgment you may turn a winning situation into a losing situation.

Here's a lesson on the drop shot.

Shiho Okada shows perfect form on the drop shot: good hustle, backswing, racquet face slightly open, good finish out front.

NICK:
Let's have a playing lesson today.

ROBIN:
Okay. I think I'm ready to handle you.

NICK:
Really try to use your brain today. Let's see if you can hit the proper stroke each and every time. You serve to start the match. Ooops. Zero–fifteen.

ROBIN:
What was that? I thought we were going to play, and you drop-shotted me right away.

NICK:
Sure. You missed your first serve. And like most people you're a little tight in the beginning of a match. I know I've told you to stay away from the drop shot early, but there is an important exception to the rule. A drop shot on a second serve can be very effective right from the start.

Just as I thought, you pushed in your second serve, and I was ready with a drop shot for a winner. Now I've put pressure on your serve. You'll be thinking that you have to get in your first serve. If you don't, you'll be worried about your second serve. Perhaps you'll take a step or two toward the net after serving, anticipating the drop shot. Now an offensive return will go by you that much faster.

ROBIN:

Nick, you're always thinking. I never thought the drop shot was an offensive weapon.

NICK:

Every shot, even the lob, can be an offensive weapon if you use it at the proper time. Save the drop shot for the moment when your opponent least expects it, and it will be effective. Last week you played a match that went three sets when you should have taken it in two. What you failed to take into account was that your opponent was overweight and did not like to run up and back. She could hit extremely well from the baseline, however, and you fell right into her trap. You tried to slug with her. During that match, the drop shot could have been used quite a bit. You could have moved her up to the net, then lobbed back over her head. Sometimes, it isn't necessary to even try for a winner on a drop shot. Your goal should be to move your opponent around.

ROBIN:

Look at that. I hit a fine drop shot that time, but you hit another drop shot back at me.

NICK:

Right. I've told you to be prepared for your opponent to return your shot down the line, but you must also take a step or two inside the baseline in case she drop-shots you back. In this situation, if you cover her drop shot, it's very effective strategy to lob over her head, forcing her back to the baseline. Now you are at the net and in position for her passing shot or her return lob.

ROBIN:

I'm beginning to understand. But is the drop shot used in doubles?

NICK:

Be careful. Two opponents are covering the court in doubles. Use the drop shot when you have pulled your opponents far out of position and when you are fairly close to the net.

ROBIN:

I see some players hit super drop shots. Their balls just clear the net, and they have lots of underspin.

NICK:

Be cautious of those shots. Players generally make too many mistakes when they try them. A shot like that requires years of practice and hitting it thousands of times. It's better to hit a solid drop shot that lets you win the point on your next shot. Don't be the one who wins a point on a drop shot and then hits her next three attempts into the bottom of the net. Remember: Open the face slightly on contact and hold the ball on your racquet as long as possible. Keep your wrist firm. Practice this shot against a backboard, or take a bucket of balls out by yourself and work on your touch.

As you've come up through junior tennis, especially if you've had a certain amount of success, you probably have been approached by equipment manufacturers interested in seeing that you use their wares. But maybe you are still relatively new to the top levels of the game. Perhaps you have not played in many national events, or have not compiled an outstanding tournament record. Free equipment is a reward that is earned. I remember when I was teaching back in the fifties in North Miami Beach, what a thrill it was when the Wilson Sporting Goods Co. would give me racquets, a pair of shoes, or a few cans of balls for my junior program. I was in heaven! Remember, this was back in the Dark Ages, when sneakers were only a few bucks and Jack Kramer racquet frames sold for $10.

Coinciding with the tremendous boom in junior tennis over the last decade came the decision by equipment manufacturers to make a concerted effort to develop allegiance to their products through promotional efforts. The "free list" was born. Companies began to put junior players on programs in which the kids received equipment. Believe me, a great deal of planning goes into these promotions. Gone are those days when equipment reps showed up at a tournament and began passing out free stuff. Equipment now is very costly. Shoes cost $50. Racquets go as high as $400. The Italian tenniswear companies sell shirts for $100. Being selected for someone's "free list" is quite an honor, one for which you should strive.

I have been associated with the Prince racquet company for some time, and I will illustrate how someone might go about obtaining equipment from such a company.

The first thing you must do is prepare a résumé that includes both personal information and data on your tennis. In the résumé, compile the following:

1. Information on the racquet you now use: its size, style and weight.
2. The years you have played junior tennis, and your complete tournament record.

3. A picture and all pertinent press clippings, if any.
4. Full identification of your teaching pro.
5. Letters of recommendation from your pro and other people (tournament officials, umpires, other players, etc.) who are highly regarded in tennis.
6. Similar letters from your teachers or others who can attest to your character and other academic activities.

Most important, enclose a personal letter telling why you want to change to the company's racquet, or, if you already are using the brand, why you are happy with it. Include the name of your district sales representative, whose recommendation probably will go a long way with the home office.

Once you send in your résumé, you can expect to hear from the company within a short period of time. Even if you are turned down, the company may still offer you several options, perhaps allowing you to purchase your equipment at a discount. If you are turned down totally, the company usually will explain why. Often this explanation is a good barometer of how others perceive your progress in the game.

Being on a "free list" is a great feeling, but there are certain responsibilities associated with it. I caution you not to become greedy over free equipment. Too many people spend their time worrying about whether they are getting free stuff rather than concentrating on their game. Sammy Giammalva, now on the pro circuit, went all through the juniors as one of the top players in this country, and it was not until his final year in the 18s that he was put on a "free list." "I never worried about it," says Sammy.

Also, be sure to turn in your old racquets to a company that sends you new ones. This rule has come about because players were taking equipment and then selling it. Don't be a person who makes it tough for the people who follow you. If tennis is going to expand and become even more popular, we need players who do not have tremendous financial resources. Companies contribute equipment in hopes of easing the financial burden on young players.

I've seen players accept equipment and then remove the logo from that equipment. Don't do it. Manufacturers expect something for their gifts. Most of all, they want exposure. Later, if you are good enough to become a professional, your manufacturers will expect that the kindness they showed you as a junior will be reciprocated.

Finally, I must point out that the United States Tennis

Association has certain guidelines covering juniors' acceptance of equipment from firms. Check with your local USTA representative for a copy of the rules, or contact the national office. Don't jeopardize your amateur standing.

There's one more thing I want to cover here. Perhaps your play in tournaments has resulted in a certain amount of press coverage. Maybe you're the local hotshot. It is important that you now develop an attitude toward public criticism and how to accept it. I have been the subject of articles in countless newspapers and magazines. National television networks have featured me and the Academy on numerous shows. I have to admit that in every instance, there was something that struck a nerve, something that touched me in a negative way. That's normal. You are always going to be sensitive, maybe oversensitive, to any article written about you. And just as you make mistakes on the tennis court, you should expect that the writer of the article also will make mistakes. He can only report the situation as he sees it, and you should realize that he can never understand you as well as you understand yourself.

Never fall into the trap of trying to satisfy your critics. It is much more important that you satisfy yourself. Don't be worried about the people on the sidelines. Concentrate on what is happening on the court. Is all the work worth it? I would say yes. It can lead to a college scholarship, the professional tour, or maybe just a free racquet—but it also can teach you to understand criticism and to learn from your mistakes, and give you the joy of competition. And don't forget the ultimate valuable lesson: You are never so good that you cannot get better.

14

TIME OUT:
Concentration
. . . One More
Time

We've all heard the phrase, "Relax, it's only a game." Whoever first said that was probably smarter than he realized, because the key to great tennis is being able to relax, to concentrate, to make the sport what it is: only a game. It sounds paradoxical—concentration through relaxation—but if you can play like you practice you will be as good as you can be.

The other day I was working with Dan Nahirny, a 16-year-old champion from Maplewood, N.J. It was a two-on-one drill, with all of the players on the baseline. "Let the racquet go on your follow-through, let the racquet do the work," I was saying to him. *Pa-pa-pow!* He hit a fabulous shot. The ball exploded off his racquet and went from baseline to baseline so fast that the player on the other side, a nationally ranked junior, missed it. He whiffed. The point is that Dan was concentrating on one small bit of technique; he was not thinking about the score, or his opponent, or whether he was winning or losing a match. He was relaxed, focused, totally committed to the here and now. The result was a wonderful shot.

All through this book we've talked about concentration. In fact, we have a little motto at the Academy: "The three Cs— Concentration for Consistency and Confidence." If you are able to keep your concentration during matches, your level of consistency will rise markedly. Make fewer errors, your confidence increases. More confidence, fewer errors. Each builds upon the other. But the important thing, the catalyst behind consistency and confidence, is your ability to concentrate.

Years ago, a funny thing happened to Torben Ulrich, the eccentric but insightful seniors Danish player, during a match at Forest Hills. A butterfly flew into his face as he prepared to hit a shot. The press asked him about it later. Quipped Torben in his inimitable style: "Was I then a man dreaming I was then a butterfly, or am I now a butterfly dreaming I am now a man?" Everybody laughed. That Torben, they thought, what a card! But I think a lot of people missed the point. To play tennis, you must divorce yourself from the real world. Occasionally, you wind up wondering what is real and what is unreal. That butterfly was intruding on Torben's world of tennis, breaking the concentration that he sought so hard to obtain.

Probably the single thing that kept Evonne Goolagong from compiling an even more outstanding record than she did was her tendency toward "walkabouts," little spells that occasionally crept into her play. Suddenly, her concentration would falter, and she would begin spraying the ball all over the court. On the other hand, it is to the credit of John McEnroe that he can have an occasional outburst on the court, regain his composure, and get right back into the match. Nothing seems to dent his concentration, even his own temper.

Considering what happened with Borg, I think every parent of a temperamental kid should default their child once in his or her junior career. I know that sounds crazy, but bad behavior must be stopped early. It can be very harmful later. Even Bjorn Borg, as I've noted, was suspended from junior tennis for a time. He admits that as a youngster in Sweden, he "was a madman," always bringing home smashed racquets. Borg had to learn concentration before he could learn consistency and confidence. Sometimes lessons are painful, but they must be learned.

Most points end because one or the other player loses concentration. Theoretically, a match, a game, even a point can go on forever. There is no time limit in tennis. If you could run down every ball, the point would never end. A common dream with people is a nightmare in which they feel as if they must run, but their legs are paralyzed. That is what happens in tennis. Fear causes you to slow down. You have to concentrate, to focus, almost to have tunnel vision in order to keep those feet moving.

Relax, it's only a game.

There are many ways to build concentration. Some even seem contradictory. You have to figure out what works best for you. For instance, Jimmy Arias, Carling Bassett, and Pam Casale have completely different approaches to maintaining concentration.

Arias: "I think only of tennis. I don't want any outside distractions."

Bassett: "I don't think at all. When I start thinking I get into trouble."

Casale: "I try to relax in the tough spots, to think of something else. I say: 'Take it easy. Everything will be okay.' I think of a song, or something like that. That might seem weird to other people, but it makes me relax."

Whatever works for you—that's the point. You have to have *some* clear, concise method that will help you concentrate. At the Academy, one of our concentration drills involves setting up targets on both sides of the court. The students on one side try to hit the targets on the other. That's what they think of, over and over—nothing else. In fact, even when they change sides of the court, they concentrate on the targets. It is important that you develop a similar routine to build your concentration. Don't think concentration is something that just "happens," like a mushroom that pops up overnight on a lawn. Golfers come off the course exhausted after an 18-hole round, even though they have done little in the way of physical exertion. Why are they so tired? Because they have been thinking for some four or five hours. Their minds have run a marathon. Train your mind the way you train your feet.

We encourage our students to develop routines off the court that will help them in this area. Some people call our techniques "visualization." The student thinks of a relaxing situation over and over, and whenever under stress, recalls that pleasurable, relaxing image.

Some people use music. They listen to a song in an informal, peaceful atmosphere, and then attempt to "hear it" in a pressure situation. Others pick out a painting and concentrate on it, trying to imagine what message the artist was trying to convey. Other students think of themselves playing a match and concentrate deeply on the ball throughout each imaginary rally. Others put themselves in a potentially distracting situation—something like a crowded room—and then try to repeat positive thoughts, paying no attention to the noise around them.

One of my fine young students is Susan Sloane, who visits

the Academy several times a year from her home in Lexington, Ky. Fritz Nau, who started Susan as a player and who has helped her to become one of the country's best in the 14-and-unders, actually has a three-times-a-week program in which Susan works on the mental side of her game. "It's been an important part of her tennis for four years, as much as hitting balls or lifting weights," says Fritz. "Being able to pay attention to what she's thinking during matches and to handle stress are what she does very well."

Susan's program includes both deep muscle relaxation and visualization techniques. The first entails reclining in a quiet room and letting a feeling of relaxation enter your muscles; the second involves encouraging your mind to develop an image of yourself on the court. According to Fritz, "Basically I want her to be able to see herself playing. I want the picture to be in vivid detail, right down to the colors. Overall, the program is just another way of adding a little discipline. You actually wind up controlling what you think."

During practice sessions, Susan never hears the sound of the ball hitting the racquet or the court. Fritz plays loud music to mask even that noise. "It makes her zero in and watch the ball," says Fritz. "The music tends to bring her to where she is hitting, but not thinking about hitting."

Similar tricks can help you in a match. For instance, if you sense that your concentration is failing during a match, perhaps it is time to throw up a few topspin "moonballs." You're like a boxer covering up on the ropes, gaining time to collect his wits. Jimmy Connors does this all the time, especially after his opponent has hit a series of fine shots. By throwing in a couple of soft strokes, those spinners that clear the net by about 15 feet, dig into the court, and head for the back fence, Connors is able to slow down the pace and get his thoughts together again. It also can disconcert an opponent who is getting grooved on hitting the ball very hard.

Because there are so many things happening in a match that you have no control over, you must make a concerted effort to control what you can. For instance, make certain that your equipment—racquet, shoes, and clothing—is just the way you like it. Don't let a string break in the middle of a match because you tried to squeeze another few hours out of a favorite racquet with frayed strings. Don't let a shoestring snap in a game because you failed to put in new shoestrings the previous night.

But let's say that something unexpected does happen. (The net fell down one time when Bjorn Borg and Roscoe Tanner were playing a match at the U.S. Open.) Good concentration is when the umpire falls over in his chair and you look up and ask, "Did I hear a let?" I don't care if you break a string, if you run out of racquets, if your shoes fall apart—with good concentration you block out what has happened and go back to play and win. I'm amazed at how often junior players will miss a shot in a tournament and then subtly let the onlookers know that someone in the gallery upset or distracted them. Hey, the better you play, the more distractions you're going to have, because the more spectators you're going to attract. So if you blame missing a shot on some onlooker, all you are saying is "I can't concentrate. I guess I'll never be good enough to play in front of people."

When you walk onto the court, your mind, just like any other piece of equipment, must be ready. Hours before the match, you should have been concentrating on what you hope to accomplish when you face your opponent, with a clear idea of that opponent's strengths and weaknesses and how you will match up against them. Try to develop a winning attitude from the moment you wake up on the morning of a match.

Every player has been in a situation in which a crucial second serve in the third-set tie breaker has caused a 13-ounce racquet to feel like a 13-pound racquet. When this happens, I encourage my students to exaggerate the follow-through on groundstrokes and to put more spin on serves, hitting through the balls. During changeovers, take deep breaths to calm yourself, and take yourself back to the visualization techniques that you used off the court.

Just as there are no right and wrong ways to hit a tennis ball, no one single concentration method works for everyone. You have to experiment and find out what is best for you, but you must find something. For without concentration, no matter how well you hit a tennis ball, you will be a loser—and very often to much poorer players.

15

THE DECISION
(Eighteen)

Well, you're near the end now, almost home. It's been a long road. Looking back, it must seem like a very long road. When you started, this time seemed so far away, and now here it is. One more decision, one more after so many. Now that you are 18, you must consider whether you want to go to college or whether you are ready to try the pro circuit.

First of all, you have to realize that there are 500 ranked men, 200 ranked women, and thousands of amateurs all trying to get through the same door on the professional circuit. If you thought competition was rough during the juniors, you're going to have your eyes opened now. Merely turning professional, no matter how outstanding your record in the juniors, in no way guarantees that you'll find the success you want. Now we begin playing for keeps.

Right off the bat, I would say that turning professional is a decision that 99 out of 100 players should delay until after they have experienced college. Why go to work now? For that's what pro tennis is, believe me—work, beyond anything you've known up to now. Yet three of my students—Carling Bassett at 15, and both Jimmy Arias and Aaron Krickstein at 16—turned professional before they finished high school, much less entered college.

There are several factors to consider. Obviously your playing record is very important. We at the Academy demanded that Carling, Jimmy, and Aaron win big against their peers before they could move up. Carling's victory in the Orange Bowl in 1982 showed that she was ready. Jimmy had proven himself on what is now the Nike satellite circuit. He had also become the youngest player in history to win a match at the U.S. Open when he won his first round in 1981. And, of course, after Aaron swept the 18-and-under circuit in '83, then beat the world's top-ranked junior, Stefan Edberg of Sweden, in a great 4½-hour match in the first round of the U.S. Open main draw, and finally defeated Vitas Gerulaitis that same week, it was apparent that he was ready for the pro circuit. The decision proved correct when he won his very first pro event.

But playing performance was only one of the factors we considered in each decision. Also considered were the respective families' financial backgrounds. It's quite a drain on parents to have to send their children all over the world to play tournaments as amateurs. Our three young stars were assured of fine sponsor contracts because of their marketability. Even if they failed to win much prize money in their early years, their income was guaranteed through equipment contracts.

Additionally, we considered the physical and mental characteristics of each. They were tough kids who had demonstrated they were fighters on the court. As a pro you have to be able to take a physical and mental beating and still have the guts to come back for more. Tracy Austin, for example, has suffered through tremendous physical problems, perhaps because she began playing the pro circuit at too young an age. Andrea Jaeger is another prodigy who is having physical problems. Don't discount the added pressure that you will encounter being so young. We hold our breath every day, hoping that our youngsters, kids such as Lisa Bonder and Pam Casale, can stay away from injuries. We emphasize the importance of continuing the stretching programs, of workouts off the court, and of a proper diet.

Sometimes, the pro life literally forces you to follow these guidelines. When Jimmy Arias turned pro, he felt he was in good shape. Early in his pro career, however, he began getting cramps. He remedied this condition through off-court conditioning, but still he was not as physically strong as I would have liked. The turning point came in the spring of '83, when he and Jimmy Brown, another young pro, were training at the Academy. "We would play and practice all day," Jimmy Arias recalls. "At the end I would be dead. And then Jimmy would go off and jog! I couldn't believe it. One day I went with him. I kept up with him for the first mile, and then he pulled away. In fact, after the second mile he had almost lapped me. But I kept at it, and within a couple of weeks I

think I was almost keeping up with him. Another month and I would have been beating him, I think." After years of listening to me harp about how he needed to work harder off the court, Jimmy finally got the message when his competitiveness made him want to keep up with Jimmy Brown. Thanks for the lesson, Mr. Brown.

Another option that is available to you now is to go out and try the Nike satellite circuit as an amateur. Arias did this when he was young and it proved a fantastic training ground for him. I compare the Nike circuit and the stages leading up to it to the training I received in the paratroops. Your first few years are like jumping off three-foot-high ledges. Then you graduate to the 34-foot tower (age-group competition). And then they put you on the 250-foot tower (the Nike circuit). At each step, fewer of your buddies move on with you. But make it past the 250-foot tower and you are ready for the real thing (pro circuit).

Carling Basset turned pro at 15. She has one of the best backhands in the world.

"Nick said to go, so I went," Arias says now, recalling his first trip to the satellite trail. "Just winning one or two matches was great. I was playing for fun. There wasn't much pressure. I wasn't even thinking about any pro computer points. I didn't even know what they were until after I got one. The thing I liked was that I was in the match against everybody. When you're in the match, you should be able to beat anybody, if you're mentally tough enough. That's what it comes down to. It seems to me that so much of tennis these days is mental. These juniors at the Academy all hit the ball great. It all comes down to the mental side. That is what the satellite circuit taught me, how to tough out a match."

Given Jimmy's success, I have to get in a little dig at my friend Arthur Ashe. From the beginning, Arthur told people we were making a mistake by allowing Jimmy to turn pro so young. Now that he has progressed to a solid performer in the top 10, however, I think even Arthur would admit that we made the right decision. However, I must reiterate: Don't turn pro without solid reasons. In America, people have always depended on having an education. Jimmy was lucky enough to get his in tennis. He learned things that he never could have picked up from books.

Still, another of my students, Eric Korita, became a successful touring professional after first attending Southern Methodist University for two years. Listen to what Eric has to say: "To me, college was a fantasy life. I was on my own. I could do what I wanted. It was a lot of fun. College was when I began to grow up. I needed to learn how to take care of myself, how to take responsibility for my tennis and for school. It was a growing experience, and one of the best times of my life. I really enjoyed it."

College taught Eric that he needed to work on his weight and his game. In his freshman season, he played no. 5 on SMU and lost a lot of matches. His weight had shot up to about 240 pounds. So over the summer, he trained and lost 40 pounds, and then in the U.S. Open that fall he fought through the qualifying rounds and won two matches in the main draw before extending Yannick Noah to five sets in the third round. But even then, Eric did not turn pro. He went back to college.

"I still needed to prove myself," he says. "I had a much better season. I played number two behind Rodney Harmon and I ended the year ranked fifth in the national collegiate standings. It started me on my way." So finally Eric turned pro, and now he is in the top 50.

Although Eric took a different route from that taken by some of my other top students, I must point out that he too played the Nike circuit and found it a tremendous learning experience. "It taught me to take my lumps," he says now. "And it gave me a lot of satisfaction. You know you can hang in there for the five weeks that each segment on the tour takes. It's hard—staying in different motels . . . staying in different people's houses . . . driving all night from city to city. My car kept breaking down. It was something."

I guess overall the message I am trying to get across is that it is important to test the water before you make a big jump. Ease on in, find out just how cold the life out there can be, and how hot the competition is.

If you decide on college, there are several guidelines you might consider when trying to figure which one is best for

Four who went to college: Tim Mayotte (1981 NCAA champion), Mike DePalmer, Chip Hooper and Lloyd Bourne.

you. The obvious question is, Who is the coach of the program? I feel strongly that if you are good enough to get a college scholarship, in all probability your game is at such a level as to have no glaring weaknesses. Now is not the time to begin making big changes. Having learned how to play, you need to find a coach who will help your game *within its present framework,* not one who will make tremendous changes. One of my students, Rodney Harmon, had a bad experience when he went off to SMU. Dennis Ralston, a great player on the pro circuit, a former Davis Cup coach, and an excellent technician, now coaches SMU. He took a look at Rodney's two-handed backhand and decided that Rodney would be better off if he hit a one-hand backhand. And it didn't work. Now, I don't say that people can't change their strokes late in their tennis careers. Australia's Paul McNamee switched from a one-hand to a two-hand backhand at 28, and the next year he beat John McEnroe in the French Open. But making the switch McNamee made—one-hand to two— and making the change that Harmon tried—two-hand to one—are very different. Which is to say that the first can be

done while the second is almost impossible. Rodney suffered during his college career because of it, and even now, playing on the pro circuit and using his old two-hand backhand stroke, he still has not recaptured his confidence.

When you consider college, you also have to think about the school's practice facilities. Roland Jaeger, the father of Andrea, has told me that Susy, Andrea's older sister, probably made a mistake by going to Stanford University, historically one of the finest tennis schools in the country. The program was great at Stanford, but the school has only hard courts, and because Susy had foot problems she wound up playing injured for most of her career.

You also have to take a look at the team members already on the squad. If they are too good, perhaps it will be difficult for you to crack the lineup. If they are not good enough, they will not offer much competition during practice. Remember, these players will be your practice partners for nine months a year.

And don't forget to factor in such things as weather, the school's practice schedule (whether it is year-round or simply seasonal), and the additional help and practice time available at local clubs.

Collegian or pro, you are going to find this final step up the ladder huge, in that the pressure under which you perform will be significantly higher. As Ken Rosewall has said, "All tennis matches are lonely." I've watched students go through this over the years, and I have a little checklist I use to help them in the tough spots.

First of all, I tell them to try and find whatever it is that helps them to play their own game. They must concentrate on what *they* want to do, not on what they think their opponents will do. It is important that you learn to play for yourself. When you started in junior tennis, chances are that you got great joy out of performing for your parents. Now you must cut loose that feeling. Learn to be your own worst critic, and learn to satisfy yourself.

I also point out that most of the pressure that comes from a match is self-inflicted by the simple fear of losing. I think you can reverse that fear. Jimmy Arias, before a big match, imagines the worst thing that can happen to him: a loss. It's not going to be the end of his career, or the worst embarrassment he has ever suffered. Just a loss. This simple thought helps to relax Jimmy.

It is also very important to be natural and relaxed when you are on the court. I see students freeze up. They fail to realize that their opponents are just as nervous. Also, they forget about keeping their breathing nice and smooth. In your first pro match, or the first time you play for your school, you probably will notice yourself breathing very quickly. Slow it down, finish the stroke completely, and keep your feet moving. If the brain dies, numbed by fear, the feet quickly follow.

One final tip. In tight spots, go for your big shots, the trademark of a winner. By hitting out, even if it's not a winner, you'll make the person on the other side of the net think a little bit. Also, hitting out keeps you from trying those difficult "touch" shots, the hardest ones to make under pressure. And slow down! Have you noticed how often, when you are in a hurry to do something around the house, you make the silliest mistakes? The same thing happens on a tennis court.

Pressure is only a word. You can learn its meaning either in the pros or in college, but the important thing is that you become acquainted with it on a personal basis. Don't fear pressure. If you have developed sound basic strokes and are in good physical condition, you can handle anything that comes. Look back at all the work you have done. Now is the time to begin to enjoy it. Education or dollars, whichever you decide. At the very least, you will have a lifetime sport. Good luck.

FOUR

Tournaments

16

PROCEDURES AND STRATEGY

I love tournaments. The day-to-day practice is the assembly line, the routine part of the game. The tournaments are where you show off the finished product. There's always something going on. The kids are out there battling, putting their souls on the line. The parents are chewing their nails. The agents are scoping out the competition. The press is interviewing people. It's action. I relish it.

All of the funny stories, all of the stuff that people remember, always happens at the tournaments. One year Steve Owens, one of my assistants, plugged his hair dryer into an electrical outlet in Rome—and blew out every fuse in the hotel. Aaron Krickstein was *attacked* by a towel rack in the men's washroom at another Italian tournament. While washing his hands, Aaron reached for a towel, and the rack fell and hit him in the head. Frustrated and angry, Aaron shoved the rack and it rebounded, hit the wall, and came back and smacked him in the face, opening a cut on the bridge of his nose. Twice wounded, Aaron decided to retreat before the towel rack could get in any more licks. TKO'd by a bathroom fixture.

Of course there is a serious side to tournament play. Tennis is a results game—it's two people fighting to win points, and the black-and-white statistics don't lie. You're only as good as your last victory. Your tournament record becomes as much a part of you as your surname.

Parents always ask me, "What tournaments should my child enter?" That's easy. City tournaments are for the novice player. State tournaments are for the advanced player. Next come sectional events, tournaments that draw entries from a three- or four-state area. Win or do well here, and you are ready for the national events. And then—get out your passports—the international circuit. Step by step. Take them one at a time.

You hear stories about players who are afraid to compete in tournaments. Lori Kosten, one of my former students, got so caught up in her late teens in recalling a triumphant past, remembering how she never lost as a girl of eight or nine years, that as other players started to catch and pass her she'd become physically ill at tournaments. She became terrified at the prospect of losing. A parent must do everything possible to see that a child keeps a positive attitude toward competition. Never criticize a child for errors. Kids may make what seem like "mental" mistakes—hitting the wrong shot, missing a setup at the net—which may in fact be caused by physical shortcomings. Parental criticism can kill a kid's will to fight faster than anything I know. Almost all kids try their best. If they don't, if they turn in a slipshod, seemingly half-hearted effort in a match, maybe it is their way of saying, "I'm sick of it."

For most kids, however, tournaments can be a great way to whet the competitive instinct. The parents of Ginny Purdy, one of my top juniors, have told me that Ginny decided as a very young girl that she wanted to be a top player after she competed against girls three and four years older and lost. Ginny seemed to be saying, "I'll come back some day and beat you." That's a fighter's attitude.

Another of my juniors, Ann Grossman, a 13-year-old who grew up on an Ohio farm—hardly where you'd expect to find a tennis talent—played her first tournament when she was six. She loved it. In fact, it was the experience that got her started as a junior. In that first event, Annie didn't even know how to keep score, or how to call balls "out." When she walked off the court, she asked her father, "Daddy, who won?" From that moment on, Ann was a tournament player. Now she is nationally ranked. She says, "I always loved the tournaments and the challenge. It was fun getting to meet people all over the United States."

I'm going to give you some pointers on the procedures for entering tournaments at the city, national, sectional, and international levels, and I'm also going to give you some strategy that might help you move up through each level. Some of the advice may seem dull, but that's just the kind of point that may prove most important to you. You don't have to

Nick with Carling Bassett and Dick Enberg of NBC at the 1983 Amelia Island WTA championship. The Academy had 12 students in the main draw.

follow this list exactly, but if you don't, you should make up your own tournament checklist and stick to it. Even an experienced airplane pilot doesn't take off without running down a list that to an outsider may seem pretty routine. Don't find yourself at 30,000 feet without a parachute . . . or a water jug to quench your thirst.

City Tournaments

1. Get your entry in on time. The entry blank will explain all the details of the tournament: dates, site, age

Yannick Noah training at the Academy.

division, entry fee, and deadline. If you have played tournaments before, you should submit your results with the entry so that you can be considered for seeding.

2. As soon as possible, figure out a plan for tournament transportation. Thousands of matches have been forfeited simply because when the time came, a player had no way to get to the event.

3. On the day before the event, call the tournament office for your match time. If you are more than 15 minutes late for your match, there's a chance you will be defaulted.

4. On the day of the event, wake at least two hours prior to your match (plus transportation time). Besides your racquets, you will need a water jug and a towel. It's also a good idea to bring along a change of clothing, and a warmup. After a match, you will stiffen up if you sit around in damp clothing. Don't forget any injury

braces you may need, and remember to bring money for lunch.

5. Watch your diet. On the night before a match, don't eat greasy foods or hard-to-digest foods such as beef. A lean dog hunts better. In the morning, a light, well-balanced breakfast, such as fruit, cereal and toast, makes a good prematch meal, but make sure you eat far enough in advance of your match so that your stomach has a chance to digest—at least an hour and a half. Food in your stomach, studies have shown, can sap your energy.

6. Stretching is a must. Because of the increased excitement your body will be under, tournament play will tax your muscles. A good warmup is essential. In all probability, practice courts will be at a premium at the tournament site, so you should think about warming up with a friend somewhere else or make arrangements for a few minutes of workout against a wall.

7. Don't be late. Leave for the tournament in plenty of time.

8. As soon as you arrive at the tournament, check in with the officials. Don't think that just because they see you they will remember you are present. Stay close to the tournament desk so you'll be available when your match is called.

9. Have your United States Tennis Association card with you. (*Hint:* You might want to make a little pocket on the inside of your racquet cover, or your tennis equipment bag, where your USTA card will fit.) That way you always will be certain to have it with you. If you are not a USTA member, check with your tennis pro about joining.

10. Find a doubles partner. If you don't have a partner prior to the tournament, ask the tournament desk to help match you with someone.

11. On the court, sportsmanship and competition go hand in hand. Don't cheat. Be sure to shake hands with your opponent—win or lose. The winner reports the score to the tournament desk. If necessary, return the match balls.

12. Start a notebook to keep a record of your tournament results—the event, the date, whom you played, and the scores.

State Tournaments

1. Entries are available through your USTA local office, the junior tennis organizations in your area, or your local tennis club. Make certain your tournament record accompanies your entry.

2. This could be your first experience with tournament "housing" if the event takes place outside your hometown. "Housing" means that a family has volunteered to host you for the time you are playing in the tournament.

3. Be certain to pack enough clothes for your stay. Remember that you'll be going through quite a few tennis outfits—especially if you play well. Don't expect your hosts also to be your private laundry. Make your bed.

4. It's a nice gesture to bring along a gift, some token of appreciation for the people who share their home with you.

5. Be thoughtful! Offer to help with some chores around the house.

6. After the tournament ends, don't forget to send a note of appreciation to your hosts.

Sectional Tournaments

1. These events are normally by invitation only. If you have done well at the state level, you can expect to receive an invitation. These tournaments, in turn, will qualify you for national events. If the tournament is listed on its entry as "open," players are eligible regardless of where they live. These tournaments are very strong. A "closed" tournament is open only to players who reside within its defined section.

2. Don't forget to advise the tournament officials of your transportation plans. Often they will arrange travel from the airport, train, or bus station to the tournament site. Be sure to inquire about housing early. If you decide to stay in a hotel, choose one near the tournament facilities.

3. Arrive one day early. You'll need time to adjust to the environment, courts, and weather.

4. If you travel by plane, it is best to take a bag you can carry aboard, one to hold your racquets, a change of clothing, and tennis shoes. If the airline misplaces your bags, you don't want to be left without equipment.

5. Bring a jump rope. Once again, there may be a problem finding practice time, and you may not want to jog in unfamiliar surroundings. Jumping rope can be a great way to loosen up.

6. Check in early at the tournament. You will receive your starting time, the name of your host family, a copy of the draw, and in all probability an information packet.

7. Try to get on the courts early, so you can find some practice time and become accustomed to the surface.

8. If you break a string, get the racquet restrung immediately. Almost every tournament will have stringing operations set up.

9. Remember, tournaments are for competition, not socializing. It is at this level that players either realize they want to excel or decide to remain good club players. Take time to be by yourself and think about your goals.

10. Don't forget to call your parents. They will be waiting to hear how you performed.

National Tournaments

1. Sectional tournaments qualify you for national play. Each section is allotted entries for national events, a quota of usually between 10 and 16 players. Do well in sectional events and you will receive a bid for national play. There are three national events during the summers, and one, the "Indoors," during the winter.

2. Remember that your entry should be returned to your sectional representative, not the national office of the United States Tennis Association.

3. Most national tournaments have an official tournament hotel. This is the hotel you should use. Always book the room for the entire week. You can cancel if you lose. Usually there are special rates for the players, so be sure to tell the hotel reservations office you are connected with the tournament. Ask for a written confirmation of your reservation.

4. Pack light. You can always do laundry. As you travel from tournament to tournament, you don't want to be bothered with a lot of luggage. You're a tennis player, not a tourist. Do not forget to bring racquet string, and special grips or racquet tape if you use them. Also, bring an extra pair of shoes.

5. Practice with different players. Practice with a purpose. Now is not the time to joke around.

6. Often there will be a chair umpire during your matches. This may be your first experience with an umpire. You'll probably get some questionable calls. Play the calls. Don't argue. Mistakes will even out.

7. There will be representatives from various racquet and clothing companies on hand. Don't get too wrapped up in their presence during the tournament. They're looking for good players, and good players don't let anything bother them the week of a tournament.

8. College coaches also will be attending, scouting the talent. If you're looking for a college scholarship, you should introduce yourself to the coaches.

International Tournaments

1. By the time you reach this level, you have tennis in your blood. Your national federation will advise you of the international schedule.

2. Don't forget your passport. Sometimes you will need a visa. Apply for one well in advance of the tournament.

3. Allow for time changes. You must arrive at the tournament city three or four days early so that you can adjust to the surroundings. Make your travel arrangements well ahead of time so that you can take advantage of cut-rate air fares.

4. Travel light. If you expect to be "housed," take a few souvenir T-shirts, preferably some with logos from United States cities and firms. These make great gifts for your hosts.

5. Bring along a dictionary to help you with the language of the country you're visiting.

6. Don't get caught in a language gap on the court. Call all of your lines loudly and with accompanying hand signals.

7. Foreign food and water can put you on the sidelines faster than a hotshot competitor. Be careful of what you eat and drink. Bottled water is a must.
8. Equipment manufacturers are very common at international tournaments. You'll be given a variety of items, so be prepared to leave with more than you came with. However, you are at a tournament to play tennis, not to get a free shirt.

The key to tournaments, whether played in Iowa City or in Hong Kong, is an understanding of strategy. All the practice, all the work means nothing if you cannot translate it into effective action on the court. Playing styles are so different and individual that people inevitably "match up" better against some players than against others. X can beat Y, Y can beat Z, but X cannot beat Z. A few years ago, Bjorn Borg had Jimmy Connors's number. Those flat, hard Connors strokes fed right into Borg's wheelhouse. He teed off and hit the ball back harder than it came. Meanwhile, John McEnroe's serve-and-volley game was a mystery to Borg. But Connors played Mac tough.

However, anytime you talk about strategy, a subject that has to be tailored to each player, there's a twofold danger. The first is that you make it too simple; chalkboard talk is cheap. The second is that you make it too complicated; while a player is still considering what to do next, it becomes what he *should have* done.

With that in mind, and knowing that the best strategy is that which you yourself devise, I am going to give you a few pointers that might solve some of the problems that confront you in tournament matches.

The no. 1 rule is to avoid errors. In every match, errors far outnumber winners, yet people insist on blasting away, trying to kill a pigeon with a bazooka. I look for safe, deep groundstrokes with a good margin of error in clearing the net. I consider "skimmers," those bullets that almost brush the net, as mistakes ready to happen. Groundstroke balls should cross the net by five to eight feet and should land within five to eight feet of the baseline.

It is important to dominate the net, the "high ground" in tennis. Control the net and you control the point. Serve and volley, if possible. Otherwise, you must come to the net on the first short ball. Follow your overheads into the net. Don't retreat. A drill we use at the Academy to drum this attacking doctrine into our players involves three balls. On the first two, the player hits groundstrokes from the baseline. On the third ball she must volley it out of the air, no matter where she is on the court, and then come to the net. It gets our students to think offensively.

Another hard-and-fast rule: When in trouble, hit crosscourt. Obviously the net is lowest at this point, and by hitting diagonally you have the additional benefit of several more feet of landing area in the corners. Hitting crosscourt is also a tremendous way to "open up" the court. If you work on your crosscourt shots and learn how to open up the court with sharp angle shots, you can make your opponent vulnerable to a shot to the big part of the court.

Understand that you and your opponent both have strengths and weaknesses. You both will be trying to probe the other's soft spot. You must hit offensive shots at every opportunity. This allows you to control the ball and prevents your foe from attacking. When you hit a defensive stroke, it allows your opponent one more chance to put a torpedo into your midsection.

When returning serve, start off by getting the ball back no matter what. As long as the match is even, continue this philosophy. Once you get ahead, however, apply pressure. Watch how often Jimmy Connors nudges out a close win in the first set, then blasts apart opponents in the second. If ahead, try teeing off on a couple of service returns.

Always try to make your opponents do what they do not want to do. If they like to volley, pin them on the baseline with deep shots. If they come in, hit at their feet. Don't be afraid to go over the top with the lob. Don't be intimidated by a big overhead. With hard hitters, you must change the pace. It was once said of former major league pitcher Stu Miller, "He has three speeds: slow, slower, and slowest." Miller struck out his share of sluggers. If you pound with a pounder you are going to get pounded.

How do you handle spin when you come up against an unorthodox player who slices and cuts the ball, a junkballer who keeps you off balance with a collection of weird shots? I suggest countering spin with spin. It's easy to match underspin to underspin, and topspin to topspin. In the first instance, the ball comes to you low, so it's not difficult to slice it back. In the second, the ball comes in at shoulder height, so it is easy to swing up and loop it back. But also think about mixing up your opponent. If you get an easy ball from a slice artist, hit a severe topspin shot back. The ball now jumps up at your opponent, which makes for a difficult return. The same thing happens when you hit a slice to a topspinner. Now the ball is low, and a topspinner has to bend extra low to get any overspin on the return.

Certain points in match play are more crucial than others. We discussed them at some length toward the close of Chapter 12—a good section to review when working out your tournament strategy.

There's no excuse for not adjusting to court surfaces. On clay, where it's so difficult to put away the ball, you must be prepared to be patient and consistent. On cement and indoors, your serve should be more of a weapon. The same holds true on grass, where flat or underspin shots are also more effective.

The wind can be a factor in your matches. Learn how to play in the wind. The smartest player and the one who concentrates the best wins in the wind. When hitting into the wind, hit with plenty of pace, height, and depth. And do not be afraid to take the net. Your opponent's passing shots may end up splattering against the back fence. When hitting with the wind, use a lot of topspin to keep the ball in play. Be aggressive and control the point from the net. When hitting in crosswinds, play down the middle, especially if in trouble. Never lob down a sideline in crosswinds. Also keep plenty of slice on the serve.

My final bit of strategy is this: When winning, don't change your overall tactics. Don't change, for example, from a serve-and-volley game into a baseline game, or vice versa. Take a few more chances to put on the pressure, but stick to your winning plan. If you're behind, analyze what needs to be done. If something fails, try it once again.

Sounds simple, doesn't it? Now if it would only work out that way, all of my students would need extra rooms just to store their silver trophies.

17

KNOW
THE RULES

Jimmy Arias gave away a chance for one of his biggest victories in 1983. It happened at the ATP Championships in Cincinnati, when Arias was playing John McEnroe. Arias got the "rope-a-dope." That's the strategy Muhammad Ali used in a big heavyweight title fight with George Foreman. Ali let his opponent tire himself out. The same thing, more or less, happened to Arias, and all because he did not know, or was not quite sure of, the rules.

To set the stage, I should tell you that earlier in the season, when Arias was playing John Fitzgerald in the French Open, Jimmy suffered a pulled abdominal muscle serving. It hurt him terribly, but officials refused to let him take an injury time-out; they ruled that Jimmy's impairment was "loss of physical condition," for which no injury time-out is allowed. Jimmy was forced to continue playing, and because it hurt him severely to serve, he had to serve underhanded. Arias went on to win the match, however.

Later in the season, he faced McEnroe in the semi-finals of the ATP Championships. It was a brutally hot day. The humidity was stifling. People were fainting in the stands. McEnroe won the first set, 6–3, but he was working hard. Under normal conditions Jimmy makes his opponents hit a lot of balls because of his quickness. Each game took a toll on McEnroe.

In the second set, Jimmy raced to a 4–1 lead, then won another game to go ahead, 5–1. Just then McEnroe walked over to the umpire's chair and said, "Call out the trainer. I need an injury time-out." He told the umpire that his back hurt.

Arias stood bewildered on his side of the court as ATP trainer Bill Norris ministered to McEnroe. Jimmy hates to stand in the sun. No matter how hot it is, he can play, but when his opponent goes into a stall and makes him stand out there with the sun beating down, it gets under Jimmy's skin. While Jimmy was wilting, McEnroe, who himself had just been on the verge of fatigue, was catching his breath on the sidelines, toweling off, taking a few drinks of water, getting a respite. He came back on the court a different player. And even though he went on to lose the second set, he cranked up in the third and ripped off a 6–0 set for the victory.

I told Jimmy later that he should have gone up to the chair and protested on the same grounds of "loss of physical condition" as had been used against him in his match against John Fitzgerald. If the officials had not heeded his complaint, it would have been interesting to see what would have happened if Jimmy had simply walked off the court. "That's what I'll do the next time," Jimmy says now. You can't blame McEnroe, on the other hand. He did what he had to do.

John Meyer, a National Chair Umpire, a USTA referee, and a friend of mine from Sarasota, has given me several situations—some common, others unusual—that might occur in a match, and the proper solution according to the rules.

Case No. 1. This hypothetical situation is similar to what happened to Jimmy Arias. In the final set, with Smith leading, 2–5, Jones serves and Smith, while returning the serve, falls to the ground clutching his calf. While Smith writhes on the ground in pain, the chair umpire inquires whether he can continue to play, but the inquiry is ignored. Smith is massaging his calf muscle, which is spasming. After almost two minutes, he arises and begins play again, winning the next three points, the game, and the match.

Solution: Smith should have been defaulted, or he should have retired from the match. Rule 30 plainly states: "No allowance may be made for natural loss of physical condition." A player who suffers cramps, or is fatigued, has only 30 seconds, the normal time allotment between points, during which to recover.

Case No. 2. In a girls 10-and-under match, Ms. Baker loses a point and bounces her racquet in frustration. It travels about eight feet. Seeing this, the assistant referee enters the court and in a fatherly manner, his arm around the youngster's shoulder, cautions the girl against throwing her racquet. Ms. Baker nods her understanding. A short time later, she loses another point, and without thinking she throws her racquet

Six of Nick's tournament stars: Pam Casale, Lisa Bonder, Aaron Krickstein, Erik Korita, Brad Gilbert, and Tim Mayotte.

again. This brings the assistant referee running onto the court. He defaults Ms. Baker.

Solution: Ms. Baker was defaulted wrongly. She had not even been warned according to the rules. The proper procedure when a racquet-throwing offense occurs is to call, "Code violation, abuse of racquet, warning Ms. Baker." If there's another offense, the same announcement is made, but now there's a penalty—loss of a point. For the third violation, the penalty is loss of game. And another violation brings a default of the match.

Case No. 3. Jones has just lost a point. He takes a ball out of his pocket and slams it against the back fence, no more than eight to ten feet away. The chair umpire says, "Code violation, abuse of ball, warning Mr. Jones."

Solution: This is an improper application of the point penalty code, since Jones has not hit the ball at a player or an official, ball boy, or spectator, or endangered anyone, and he has not hit the ball out of the enclosed court. He should approach the chair and explain that his actions were not a punishable offense according to the point penalty code.

Case No. 4. While Jones is setting up to smash an overhead, a ball from an adjacent court flies over the fence and bounces on his opponent's, Smith's, side. Smith calls "let" just as Jones hits a winning smash.

Solution: The point is replayed. This is an exception to the general rule that no point ever should be replayed. In this instance, however, Smith was correct in calling "let."

Case No. 5. Smith's second service ticks the top of the net and carries back to hit Jones on the fly.

Solution: A let is played, even though the ball did not bounce in the service box. Smith serves again.

Case No. 6. Ms. Baker serves a fault, but her opponent, Ms. Brown, returns the serve, breaking a racquet string in the process. Ms. Brown stops play, hurries to the sideline, and retrieves a new racquet.

Solution: Ms. Baker gets another first serve because of the interruption.

Case No. 7. After a series of four offenses committed by Jones, the chair umpire defaults him and awards the match to Smith.

Solution: Jones is allowed an appeal to the tournament referee who can either uphold or overturn the default.

Case No. 8. A doubles match. Smith and Jones are receiving serve. Their opponents have been scoring aces by serving down the middle. To counteract this, Smith, the receiver's partner, decides to stand *on* the center line, a foot or two inside the service line. The opponents protest, claiming interference.

Solution: Smith is within his rights under the rules. He may stand anywhere to return serve, even within the service box. If, however, he is hit on the fly with the serve while standing there, his team loses the point.

Case No. 9. Ms. Baker returns a close serve of Ms. Brown. After several exchanges, Ms. Brown wins the point. However, Ms. Baker claims the original serve was out, and she circles a mark on the clay court to verify her claim.

Solution: Ms. Brown wins the point as played. Ms. Baker needed to make her "out" call before her opponent played her return.

Case No. 10. Two players are involved in a furious match. At 30–15 in the fourth game, they realize that they have forgotten to change ends at the conclusion of the previous game.

Solution: Change at once. All points stand as played. Then change again after every odd game for the rest of the set.

Case No. 11. Ms. Baker, in a Girls' 16 match, decides she doesn't need the rest period after she and Ms. Brown have split the first two sets. Instead, she wants to stay on the court and practice her serve.

Solution: She must seek permission from the referee to use the match court. In no case may she use the match balls to practice.

Did you know that the player winning the toss of the coin at the start of the match has the option either to choose one end of the court, *or* to serve or receive? Did you know that if a server breaks a string on the first serve and it's a fault, he is not entitled to another first serve after getting another racquet?

It is TRUE that at the completion of a 12 point tie break, players always change ends. If the score is 7–6, you change ends on the odd game. It is TRUE that a ball passing below the level of the net outside the net post, but landing safely in an opponent's court, is a properly played stroke. It is FALSE that you may be defaulted after a third penalty has been assessed against you. It is FALSE to think you cannot be defaulted for lateness, once the match has begun. After an authorized intermission, such as a rain delay, if court and opponent are ready to play, you'll be penalized if you are late for the resumption of play: loss of game for being up to five minutes tardy, default for more than five minutes.

These are just several of the situations that can come up when you are playing in a tournament. Because junior tennis is a loosely administered sport, one in which the players often have to make their own rules interpretations, it is important to know the regulations. Every player needs a copy of a USTA publication *A Friend at Court*. It contains the official rules of tennis, tournament regulations, and "The Code" and its 43 guidelines for non-umpired matches. Contact USTA Publications, 729 Alexander Rd., Princeton, NJ 08540.

AFTERWORD

I have tried to give you my formula for success, the one I have used over the years for myself and my students. Work hard, and the rest comes easy. Work hard and you can be satisfied with yourself.

All the great ones have it: that desire to be the best they can. Think of Pete Rose in 1984, working out on Nautilus machines during the off-season in anticipation of playing baseball for the Montreal Expos at the age of 43. Pete Rose never shortchanged himself. Nor did Bjorn Borg, Jimmy Connors, or Chris Evert Lloyd. And look at all it got them.

Jim Tressler is a young instructor at the Academy. He played college tennis and coached for a couple of years before joining us. When he got here, he was amazed at the quality of play from our juniors. On every court—*pa-pa-pow*—like magic. Said Jim, "Nick, how do they get so good?"

"Just watch," I told him. "You'll see."

There's a French junior at the Academy, John Fleurian, a youngster who fought his way through the qualifying round and made it all the way to the semifinals of the Orange Bowl juniors tournament in 1983. He did it all on his own. He was not even on the team the French Tennis Federation picked for international juniors competition. He paid his own way, and fought his own battles. He is my kind of guy, a hard worker in a factory of hard workers. Fleurian is first up in the mornings, out on the courts practicing his serve. And at night, after dinner, he comes back for more.

One Sunday, a day of rest for Academy kids, Jim Tressler walked out of his room at 7:00 A.M. and looked out on the running track. It was a clear day, the sky warmed to blue by the morning sun. On the track was a lone figure doing roadwork, his feet digging up little clumps of sand, his breath coming in spurts, like a locomotive. It was Fleurian, the man without a tennis federation behind him, getting an early start on another day of labor.

A few hours later Jim Tressler told me the story. Then he added, "Nick, now I know how they get so good."

I love it. We've got the numbers. From numbers come good players. From good players come great players. We're on a roll, and it will continue to snowball, because we do it right. A few weeks ago I was talking to someone and they asked me how things at the Academy were going. I said, "Things are going so great that I'm thinking of starting my own country, er . . . company." Maybe it was a slip of the tongue, but maybe my subconscious was trying to tell me something. I know that we are an emerging nation of tennis players, a force to be reckoned with. Up in our indoor center, we have pennants hanging from the ceiling that list the tournaments won by our players. Someone said it looked like all those Celtic championship banners hanging in the Boston Garden. That's fine with me. I don't mind being compared to the most successful franchise in sports.

I think back over the years . . . Starting out in Miami Beach, wondering what someone meant when they asked me to show them an Eastern Forehand; traveling with Brian Gottfried, hoping that we would get to the next tournament before the sun set so we might have a few minutes of practice; moving from job to job like a tennis vagabond, playing my tune for whoever would listen. There were a lot of tough times in there, but I kept working for what I believed in. I kept knocking on the door.

Down in Dorado Beach, there were periods when we were flooded with tourists, but there were other times, usually late in the season, when the courts were empty. During those periods, I could go days without seeing a player, much less teaching a lesson. There was a road at the resort that ran down from the hotel to the tennis courts, and my wife and I would sit in the shop, one eye on the road. If ever we saw someone walking down it, we would grab our racquets and race out onto the court and begin playing . . . just to make our situation look better for a passing tourist.

I always wanted to be a champion, but the hourglass ran out on my athletic career. So I channeled my energy in another direction. If I couldn't do it on the court, I'd help others do it. I remember back almost 20 years ago, talking with Donald Dell, then a young lawyer fresh off the tennis circuit. Back then, tennis was a nice little game that the gentry kept more or less in its back pocket. A few of the stars made money with under-the-table payments, but for everyone else the game was not much more than a chance to get a suntan.

The faces of Nick Bollettieri.

Donald Dell told me he had an idea. He wanted to start a professional circuit on which anyone and everyone could compete for prize money. His idea eventually became today's Grand Prix circuit. I listened to Donald as he talked of his dream. And I thought of my own dream: building a tennis academy for kids, a training center to which youngsters from around the world could come and learn to be great. Donald's dream came true. Mine did too, it just took a little longer.

In the early years, when we started at the Colony with our small group of pioneer students, I knew we had something going. I was like a football coach rebuilding for the future. My protégé, Brian Gottfried, was gone, and now I was building a stable of new champions. I knew we could make our operation into something big. Ten students. Then 25. Then 50. We kept multiplying. But not enough people knew about us. We needed to get out the word.

One time I heard that American Express was going to have a small business meeting at the Colony. This was our chance! American Express's "Do you know me?" commercials were just starting to be shown on television. I gathered together the students and my assistants, Steve Owens and Chip Brooks. I got out the videotape camera, and we filmed our own commercial! I was on the court teaching. Jimmy Arias and Carling Bassett were on the sidelines yelling, "C'mon Nick. We're late. We have to go!" They ran onto the court, gathered up our bags, and off we went. Walking away, I turned to the camera and held up a credit card. "Don't leave home without it," I said. We sent that commercial to American Express. Never heard back from them.

So we bombed in that publicity effort, but slowly the word started to filter out. Bollettieri's team was moving up. The kids were doing well. You could see their names climbing up the tournament draw boards. More and more wins. Better and better. We kept going, on our way to no. 1.

A few years ago, I was absolutely thrilled when asked to appear on a panel of coaches that included Harry Hopman, the coach of the Australian Davis Cup teams that ruled tennis during the 1950s; Vic Braden, another renowned authority on tennis; and Dennis Van der Meer, recognized as one of the game's fine teachers. Here I was, Nick Bollettieri (that's two *l*s and two *t*s), the guy who never won a tournament in his life, the old paratrooper who never grew out of being a kid, up there with the big guys. I loved it.

People say, "Nick, why don't you slow down?" I look at them like they're crazy. Slow down? Why, I'm having the time of my life. This is the fun part. Teaching kids how to be great, how to concentrate, how to set goals and through dedication and diligence attain them and achieve something worthwhile—that's what I do best.

Every day, along about 11:30 in the morning, I have a little ritual. I get my lawn chair, walk out in front of my office, and settle back into the shrubbery for about 15 minutes of sun. I look forward to this period. It's my daily dose of relaxation. Usually while I'm sitting there, a few students walk by. We'll talk. Likely as not, each youngster will have a small problem. A kid's life is nothing but a compilation of small problems. Maybe they can't play in the tournament they want, or perhaps their new racquets haven't arrived. Stuff like that. As the youngster walks away, I'm yelling to my secretary, Kathy Owens, to get me Gabe Jaramillo or Tim Kelty or Ted Meekma, my top assistants, so that we can handle the problem. No lists. No let's-take-care-of-it-tomorrows. Get it done! Now!

One day, someone observed this little tableau. "Gee Nick," the guy said. "Every time you talk to a kid, another problem comes up." I told him that's the way I like it. I want to have problems. I want to take care of little things. Take care of the little things and you never have to worry about the big things. That's what I've tried to get across to you in this book. Don't let things slide. Don't do things halfway. You can make it. It's a race you can win. But you have to do it right.

I've given you the program, the same one we use at the Academy. You've got the basics, the drills, the conditioning, the philosophy. You've got everything our students have, including me. I want to be part of your life in some way. I want you to think of Nick when you are working toward your dream. Think of me, and what I had to do for my dream, when those days crop up when you just don't want to do the work, those days when it all gets too boring and tedious. I've been there.

You can be as good as you want to be. I did it, and so can you. If you keep working, and keep trying, if you're willing to do whatever is necessary to get there, you will succeed. It has to happen. Someday, you can play at Wimbledon, *if* you really want it. And I'll be there, waiting. Don't let down Nick, and you won't let down yourself. That's a promise.

APPENDIX:

Nutrition Questions and Answers

by Ann Quinn

What should a sound nutritional diet for tennis players consist of?

Food provides our bodies with the necessary nutrients for efficient functioning. A sound nutritional diet must be balanced with a variety of foods. The daily essential nutrients, vitamins, and minerals can be obtained in the four food groups outlined below. Be sure that your diet includes all these food groups, since a deficiency in any one can mean trouble on the court.

1. Meat (2 servings+) — meat, fish, poultry, nuts, peas, beans.
2. Dairy foods (2 servings+) — milk, cheese, yogurt, ice cream.
3. Bread/Cereals (4 servings+) — bread, cereal, rice, spaghetti.
4. Fruits and vegetables (4 servings+) — apples, oranges, salads, potatoes, corn.

The number of servings listed (per day) will supply only essential nutrients, and they represent a balanced diet. Extra servings containing extra calories will be required to meet full training needs.

What about prior to a match? What is suitable for a prematch meal?

1. The best prematch meal is high in carbohydrates—for "ready energy"—and low in fat, with plenty of liquids. Some examples of appropriate foods for inclusion in a pregame meal are fish, lean meats, cooked vegetables, potatoes, bread, cereals, biscuits, lean meat and salad sandwiches, fruit punch, pancakes, waffles, spaghetti.
2. Avoid food high in fats and protein on the day of competition. Fats will only slow the digestion of the stomach. Proteins (including the traditional pregame steak) can inhibit the elimination of waste products produced by the muscles during exercise.
3. Pregame meals should be eaten three to four hours prior to a match, in order to prevent discomfort or gastrointestinal upset. Overeating should definitely be avoided. The food should be gastrically nonirritating and pleasant tasting.
4. Although the prematch meal is important, your performance will depend more on your diet over the rest of the week.

Many of my friends eat chocolate bars prior to matches. Is this good for you?

Candy bars do *not* provide "quick energy." Chocolate is essentially a fat and is slow to digest (4–6 hours). Also, sugar contained in candy draws fluid from the body into the gastrointestinal tract . . . causing premature dehydration and diminished performance.

What about during a match?

A tennis match or practice session may go on for hours. Also, any serious tennis play must deal with heat and humidity sooner or later. Thus, fluid intake is very important to ensure maximum performance.

The following rules should be observed:

1. What you drink should not be excessively cold. Ice-cold water can cause contractions in the muscles of the wall of the stomach, causing cramps and gastric pain.
2. The drink should not lead to thirst. Such glucose products as Gatorade are okay. Water is ideal. At NBTA matches, all players are required to bring a water jug.

3. The liquid should not be fizzy, or gaseous. This produces gastric distentions and, again, feelings of discomfort.

4. You should not drink too great a quantity during the match. Your motto should be, "Little and often." Actually, tennis is very fortunate in that the 1½-minute break allowed at the change of ends is just enough for such replenishment and ensures regular and frequent replacement of lost water.

Does it matter at all what I have after a match?

1. Most players don't feel like eating soon after a match, but a period of rest and relaxation will result in the appetite returning more quickly. That is because it takes some time for the body to revert back to its readiness to digest food after vigorous activity.

2. Be sure to replace lost fluids, but not too hastily.

3. The postmatch meal can be any palatable, good-sized, balanced meal, but it should not involve any great intake of fats. A good quantity of carbohydrates replenishes one's reserves.

How can I determine my ideal weight?

Height-weight charts are not especially accurate. They are derived from measurements of a great number of people. Although such charts enable each person to make comparisons with the average male or female, they are often inadequate guides to normal weight. Most athletes who are low in body fat but very muscular would be overweight according to these charts. Undoubtedly, the proportion of fat tissue on your body determines your proper weight. This can be estimated by the use of skin-fold calipers, and the proper percentages should be as follows:

SEX	AVERAGE	OBESE	ATHLETES
Male	13.5–17%	20%	7–10%
Female	20 –24%	27%	14–17%

How do I go about getting to this ideal weight, if I am carrying a few too many pounds?

Dieting is very much a gradual process. I don't recommend a loss of more than 2–3 pounds per week (7000–10,500 calories). Losing weight more rapidly results in a burning off of water and lean muscle mass, not fat.

Here at the Academy, we have our own Weight Watcher's Club that meets three times a week, and as all students live in, we can monitor their food intake. We lose pounds by working with two principles: (1) decreasing food intake and (2) increasing physical activity. We also religiously count calories and keep a notebook of everything eaten.

Maintenance of one's proper body weight is most important to optimum performance. Sudden crash diets and the use of high-protein shakes as a substitute for meals are not the answer. Many such diets recommend daily calorie intake to be as low as 600 calories per day. This may be sufficient for a sedentary person, but for a tennis player, training hard and participating in tournaments, such a diet is unwise and unhealthy. Those 600 calories would be burnt up in just over an hour in a tough practice, thus leaving a player with no energy.

Being overweight results from taking in a greater number of calories than is necessary for exercise and basal metabolism. The excess is stored as fat and results in weight gain. Five hundred unburned calories each day will result in one pound of weight gain per week (1 lb. fat = 3500 calories). When on a diet, one's calorie intake should never drop below 1200 calories per day for females, and not less than 1500 calories per day for males. A balanced, nutritious diet is essential to retain health and energy while reducing.

It is also very important to stress here that three meals a day is a must. Almost always, skipping a meal results only in overeating at the next meal. Food such as donuts, pastries, cookies—all the goodies from the snack machines, desserts, soft drinks, and so forth—should be cut out altogether. Also, no second helpings. This habit of sensible eating and regular exercise will prevent the "roller-coaster syndrome" of gaining, dieting, losing, and regaining.

Are there some hints you could give me to lose some of these pounds?

1. Eat a light meal in the evenings.
2. Eat slowly and chew thoroughly.
3. Avoid second helpings.
4. Eat low-calorie snacks only—celery, carrots, etc.
5. Don't eat between meals.
6. Always count your calories—know those foods high in calories and avoid them. (A calorie chart can be found in most nutrition books, health books, or cookbooks.)

What about the more fortunate among us who need to gain weight?

How lucky you are! The following guidelines will help produce desirable gains in muscle weight (as opposed to fat weight). Skinfold thickness should be evaluated regularly.

1. Calorie intake should be equal to or slightly greater than the body's caloric need. This can be achieved by eating an extra helping of each food or by eating snacks. Some people prefer 5–7 frequent small meals to eat more and thus not feel bloated.

2. Engage in weight training. This will promote muscular growth for added body weight.

3. Conserve energy. Living at a rapid pace with little time for relaxation prevents the efficient utilization of the diet. Slow your tempo of living, get more rest and sleep, and reduce unnecessary physical activity.

4. Consume a wide variety of foods.

5. Go for the calories. Blender drinks help provide extra calories. This is very important during intensive training. Such foods as ice cream, milk, fruits, honey, and peanut butter can be easily blended to make tasty milk shakes that can be taken several times a day in addition to the regular meals.

Because my schedule is so hectic and I'm often running late to go to practice, I usually just skip breakfast. Does this matter very much?

Skipping breakfast, whether because one is running late or just not feeling hungry, is very common. However, a tennis player who skips this meal will hamper his or her performance. Before breakfast, the body's blood sugar is low, and this decreases muscular efficiency. If breakfast is not eaten, this lack of muscle efficiency can lead to a condition known as hypoglycemia, the symptoms of which are fatigue, headache, nervousness, irritability, depression, and dizzy spells. Also, skipping this meal will deprive the body of the necessary nutrients that have been depleted during the evening and sleeping hours.

Is there a required number of hours I should sleep every night to ensure a good performance?

Your own body is the best determinant of how many hours' sleep you should have. Eight hours is normal for junior players, though this will vary with age—more sleep the younger you are, less as you get older. Adequate sleep and rest are essential prerequisites for maximum performance. The tissue building and repair process so vital in athletes, especially at the time of intense training or important tournaments, occurs principally during sleep and rest. As a general rule, heavy training and competition schedules necessitate more sleep than a sedentary life-style. This permits full physical and mental restoration of one's body.

INDEX